AIHPC® Cloud

AIHPC: ARTIFICIAL INTELLIGENCE CYBER CLOUD PLATFORM

– CLOUD AI CYBER 350

AIHPC® Cloud

AIHPC® Cloud

AIHPC® Cloud

AIHPC® Cloud

Section 1: AIHPC PaaS

1. What is Artificial Intelligence (AI)?

Recently human intelligence such as learning and problem solving has been quickly approached by machine computing. The notion of Artificial Intelligence (AI), also known as machine intelligence, may be substantiated by the fast-moving machine learning technologies that have started the next industrial revolution.

2. What is Machine Implicit Learning (MIL)?

Extended from human learning, machine learning technologies include a family of classification algorithms. Human implicit learning refers to a set of classification capabilities acquired without human awareness.

Can one train machines to acquire implicit learning capabilities from studying images based on machine learning?

The AIHPC 202 book documents the problems and solutions to develop the machine implicit learning capability of image machine learning by using AIHPC cloud that integrates top machine learning technologies.

3. What is AIHPC cloud platform?

AIHPC (AI and HPC) cloud is a next-generation Amazon cloud paltform of machine intelligence platforms (including TensorFlow and MXNet), Big Data container platforms, and cloud container computing. With a *unified user interface*, AIHPC cloud supports artificial intelligence (AI) computing and advanced cloud container infrastructure with HPC (high-performance computing) and Big Data workload.

TRAINING NOTES

4. How to launch AIHPC servers in GovCloud?

In the EC2 launch site of AWS GovCloud management console, you may search the GovCloud marketplace for "AIHPC" and launch an AIHPC server in the GovCloud (US) region. AIHPC is certified on regulated workload and sensitive data by AWS GovCloud for U.S. persons thus works best for U.S. government users.

For industrial users, you may go to the typical AWS marketplace at https://aws.amazon.com/marketplace/pp/B01JJ31R8C to launch an EC2 instance of the AIHPC cloud.

5. How to provision your AIHPC cloud cluster?

1) Launch the AIHPC AMI from the AWS link to an EC2 instance and obtain {Your IP/DNS}

2) SSH into the new EC2 and verify that "/home/ubuntu/lb.sh" launches 5 docker containers and a container load balancer

3) Open /home/ubuntu/ML_notes for instructions to test ML platforms on a universal user interface

TRAINING NOTES

6. What are the machine learning (ML) platforms integrated in AIHPC?

1) TensorFlow - Google ML platform

2) MXNet – Deep Learning Framework

3) MLR – Machine Learning in R framework

4) Weka for ImageJ

5) OpenCV

7. How are these ML platforms integrated?

These ML platforms are integrated on the R console. They are also accessible from the web client of the RStudio Server of your EC2 instance.

8. How to test integrated ML platforms from R?

SSH into your EC2 instance, then

```
1) sudo R -> source("mnist.R",echo=TRUE)

2) sudo R -> source("mxnet.R",echo=TRUE)

3) sudo R -> source("mlr.R",echo=TRUE)
```

TRAINING NOTES

9. What are the key values of AIHPC cloud?

The integrated AIHPC cloud platforms:

1) Develop new AI capabilities such as implicit machine learning

2) Provide a unified user interface to use popular ML platforms

3) Speed up your AI demo and AI solutions by providing a convenient and powerful starting point

4) Allow quick and handy ML demos from Web

5) Process machine learning and computer vision workload with the integrated AIHPC artificial intelligence platforms (TensorFlow, MXNet, Weka, ImageJ, and OpenCV3)

6) Process Big Data workload with the integrated AIHPC Spark and Hadoop container platforms and HPC cloud clusters

7) Engage container parallel processing for dockerized cloud HPC node 5 times faster than a regular EC2 host; building on the ZDAF AMI with dual-layer security for DOS and ZeroDay defense

10. Who are the users and customers of AIHPC?

1) Users: faculty and students of Cognitive Science, Computer Science and Information Management, Chief Technology Officers (CTO), Solution and Enterprise Architects, Data Scientists, and AI Sales Engineers.

2) Customers: universities, research and training institutes, consulting firms, banks, technology companies, government agencies, and other large/medium/small companies

TRAINING NOTES

11. How to access AIHPC cloud from Web?

ADC Servers	Protocol	IP Address	Port	Launch/Access
AIHPC RStudio	http	EC2 Public IP	**8787**	**ubuntu**
AIHPC Jupyter	https	EC2 Public IP	**8888**	**./jup_start &**

Note: You many want add incoming rules to the AWS security group for the EC2 instance to open the ports to trusted source IPs.

12. How to use the R Web of AIHPC cloud?

URL: http://{Your Public IP}:8787 -> user=ubuntu; password by "sudo passwd" via SSH

TRAINING NOTES

13. How to use the Jupyter Web of AIHPC cloud?

URL: https://{Your Public IP}:8888 -> click "Log in"

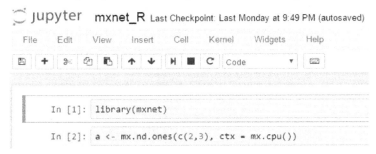

TRAINING NOTES

AIHPC® Cloud

14. How to create HPC clusters with AIHPC AMI?

1) Use AWS CfnCluster {see instruction at https://aws.amazon.com/hpc/cfncluster} custom_ami={AIHPC AMI ID};

2) Use MIT StarCluster {see instruction at http://star.mit.edu/cluster} node_image_id={AIHPC AMI ID}

15. How to locate the {AIHPC AMI ID} for a specific region to build HPC clusters?

AIHPC AWS Product Page -> Continue -> Manual Launch -> AMI IDs for different regions

TRAINING NOTES

16. How to launch 5 Docker containers and a container load balancer?

/home/ubuntu/lb.sh {execute this script from SSH command line}

17. Why is your HPC cluster on AIHPC AMI 5 times faster?

With AIHPC cloud, the additional 5 Docker containers are running in parallel to expand the processing power. This makes your HPC cloud 5 times faster than conventional EC2 instances that do not use AIHPC.

18. Can AIHPC reduce the number of EC2 worker nodes?

Yes. With AIHPC cloud, each of the 5 containers of a worker node can process similar workload as an original worker node.

TRAINING NOTES

19. What is the URL to verify that the load balancer is working for a worker node?

Browser -> http://{Your IP/DNS}:9000/

20. How to show the 5 containers and the enterprise load balancer on EC2?

docker ps {this also verifies that the load balancer are running for the 5 containers}

TRAINING NOTES

21. How to use the computer vision AI platform on AIHPC cloud?

Using an SSH session, go to the folder:

~/opencv-3.0.0/OpenCV_3_KNN_Character_Recognition_Python

1) Use the windows remote desktop client and log in to your EC2 instance.

2) Open file manager -> Tools -> Open Current Folder in Terminal

3) cd ~/opencv-3.0.0/OpenCV_3_KNN_Character_Recognition_Python

4) python TrainAndTest.py {Test 1}

5) python GenData.py {Test 2}

TRAINING NOTES

22. How to run face recognition on a sample Obama image?

1) cd ~/opencv-3.0.0/obama_face;

2) python t1.py haarcascade_frontalface_default.xml obama-phone.jpg;

3) cd /tmp; w3m obama-phone.jpg.faces.jpg

4) You need to use GUI to view the graphic result.

23. How to train new classifiers on images?

1) Use the windows remote desktop client and log in to your EC2 instance.

2) Open file manager -> Tools -> Open Current Folder in Terminal

3) cd ~/Fiji.app

4) ./ImageJ.sh

5) Fiji (ImageJ) menu -> Plugins -> Segmentation -> Trainable Weka Segmentation -> ~/Fiji.app/images -> obama-phone.jpg

6) Select face -> add to class 1 -> select background -> add to class 2 -> click train classifier

TRAINING NOTES

AIHPC® Cloud

24. How to run the Hadoop container platform?

```
$ docker run --privileged -it -p 50070:50070 -p 8032:8032 dc_hadoop
/etc/bootstrap.sh –bash
```

25. How to verify Hadoop UI?

browser -> http://{Your New IP}:50070/

26. How to use the Spark container platforms?

1) run spark container

```
$ docker run --privileged -it -p 8088:8088 -p 8042:8042 -p 4040:4040 -h
sandbox dc_spark bash
```

2) verify spark UI: browser -> http://{Your New IP}:4040

3) test Spark {inside spark container shell}

run the spark shell

```
pyspark {python spark-shell}
spark-shell
```

27. How to secure Hadoop container with ADD?

```
$ docker run --privileged -it -p 50070:50070 -p 8032:8032 dc_hadoop
/etc/bootstrap.sh -bash

$ source /root/.bashrc
```

28. How to secure Spark container with ADD?

```
$ docker run --privileged -it -p 50070:50070 -p 8032:8032 dc_hadoop
/etc/bootstrap.sh -bash

$ source /root/.bashrc
```

TRAINING NOTES

29. How to use GUI to view images on EC2 host?

1) make sure lxdm is running from EC2 console {i.e., the SSH session}

2) `sudo start lxdm`

3) make sure you know ubuntu password {use "sudo passwd" to reset}

4) `sudo passwd ubuntu` {in case the password for ubuntu is not set}

5) start the windows remote desktop client and enter the public DNS or the elastic IP of your server instance and hit connect.

6) enter the username (ubuntu) and password (pass) of the server instance and hit ok

7) use GUI file manager to navigate to /tmp, click obama-phone.jpg.faces.jpg

30. How to run license plate code with OpenCV3?

1) cd ~/opencv-3.0.0/OpenCV_3_License_Plate_Recognition_Python

2) Use the windows remote desktop client and log in to your EC2 instance.

3) Open file manager -> Tools -> Open Current Folder in Terminal

4) cd ~/opencv-3.0.0/OpenCV_3_License_Plate_Recognition_Python

5) python Main.py {Test 1}

TRAINING NOTES

31. What is human image implicit learning (HIIL)?

The notion of human intelligence as learning may be extended by human implicit learning research. George Miller and Arthur Reber of Harvard started the field of human implicit learning in Cognitive Science by inventing the human task of artificial grammar learning in 1960s.

There are generally two phases in artificial grammar learning experiments:

Phase 1 - training: subjects study a string of letters, all of which follow the rules of an artificial grammar.

Phase 2 – assessment of classification: the subjects are told to **classify** new strings as either following the rules of the grammar or not. The results usually show that the subjects are able to classify the strings more accurately than chance would predict. However, when asked to **clarify** why they chose to classify particular strings in as grammatical, subjects were typically unable to verbalize how they did it.

Extending the artificial grammar implicit learning research, in a human image implicit learning (HIIL) experiment (Yang and Ye, 1993), subjects are asked to classify face pictures on salient (front vs. leaning faces) and non-salient (pretty vs. not-pretty faces) dimensions after training/studying similar pictures without explicit explanation of the rules to classify the pictures. Results show that the subjects can learn implicit rules (**not able to reason why**) to **classify** new pictures better than others who do not have the implicit training.

References:

Miller, G.A. (1958). "Free recall of redundant strings of letters." Journal of Experimental Psychology. 56 (6): 485–491.

Reber, A.S. (1967). "Implicit learning of artificial grammars." Verbal Learning and Verbal Behavior. 5 (6): 855–863.

Yang, Z. L. and Ye, G. W. (1993), "Characteristics of Implicit Learning: Learning Capability and Density of Transmission and Storage," Psychological Science, 16(3), 138-161.

TRAINING NOTES

32. What is machine image implicit learning?

Machine implicit learning (MIL) falls in the intersection between cognitive science, cognitive computing, AI, machine learning, and computer vision etc.

From human subjects to AI machines as the AIHPC cloud machines, our machine image implicit learning experiment may mimic the ANOVA (analysis of variance) design of the classical human image implicit learning study (Yang and Ye, 1993) as follows:

Material of experiments: face images

Subjects: humans as students

Design: 2x2 ANOVA design

IVs = A and B

A = training factor = implicit learning/training vs. control (no learning)

B = dimension factor = salient vs. non-salient classification of images

DV = classification performance of grouping pictures

Task = image classification: ask students to group pictures to four categories. The pictures are pre-classified by complex rules that are designed to be difficult to reason yet can be learned implicitly through training.

TRAINING NOTES

33. Compare human implicit learning to MIL tasks

Human implicit learning and MIL may be compared to show many similarities except for subjects. We shall demonstrate that machines shall classify pictures implicitly better than chance.

Components	Human Image Implicit Learning (HIIL)	Machine Image Implicit Learning (MIIL)
Notion of learning (same)	Two phases: training and assessment of learning	Two phases: training and assessment of learning phases
Notion of "implicit" (same)	Humans cannot reason the complex rules of grouping	Machines cannot reason the complex rules
Subjects (different)	*Humans* such as students	Machines such as *AIHPC cloud*
Learning Material (same)	Face pictures of different classes	Pictures of different classes (e.g., cats vs. dogs)
Rules of grouping (same)	Grouping by complex rules of the classes	Grouping of pictures by complex rules of the classes
Assumption (same)	Humans can learn implicit rules to classify pictures	AI machines can learn implicit rules to classify pictures
Conclusion (same)	Humans classify pictures implicitly better than chance	*MIIL effect: machines shall classify pictures implicitly better than chance*

TRAINING NOTES

34. How to prepare the MIIL experiment?

1) MIIL stands for Machine Image Implicit Learning

2) Launch AIHPC cloud and establish an SSH session

3) Download the code from the github repo

```
git clone https://github.com/yeswici/image_keras
```

4) RStudio URL: http://{Your Public IP}:8787 -> user=ubuntu; password by "sudo passwd ubuntu" via SSH

5) Use RStudio Web to open ~/image_keras/R/MIL.R

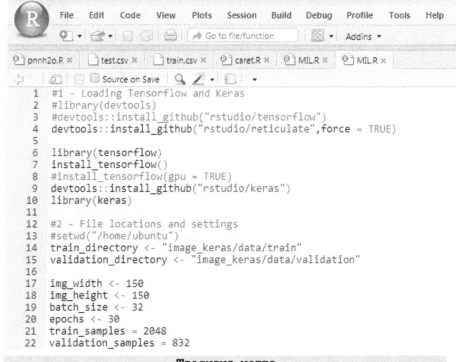

```
1   #1 - Loading Tensorflow and Keras
2   #library(devtools)
3   #devtools::install_github("rstudio/tensorflow")
4   devtools::install_github("rstudio/reticulate",force = TRUE)
5
6   library(tensorflow)
7   install_tensorflow()
8   #install_tensorflow(gpu = TRUE)
9   devtools::install_github("rstudio/keras")
10  library(keras)
11
12  #2 - File locations and settings
13  #setwd("/home/ubuntu")
14  train_directory <- "image_keras/data/train"
15  validation_directory <- "image_keras/data/validation"
16
17  img_width <- 150
18  img_height <- 150
19  batch_size <- 32
20  epochs <- 30
21  train_samples = 2048
22  validation_samples = 832
```

TRAINING NOTES

AIHPC® Cloud

35. How are images trained with AIHPC CPUs?

The MIL.R code runs on AIHPC cloud with either CPU or GPU configurations. By default, CPU is used to train the MIL AI model machine with hundreds of training images.

```
#4 - Small Conv Net - 2) training
model %>% fit_generator(
  train_generator,
  steps_per_epoch = as.integer(train_samples/batch_size),
  epochs = epochs,
  validation_data = validation_generator,
  validation_steps = as.integer(validation_samples/batch_size),
  verbose=2
)

2017-07-03 17:28:03.577623: W tensorflow/core/platform/cpu_feature_guard.cc
structions, but these are available on your machine and could speed up CPU
86s - loss: 7.8716 - acc: 0.4946 - val_loss: 7.9353 - val_acc: 0.5000
Epoch 2/30
80s - loss: 7.6510 - acc: 0.5034 - val_loss: 6.6104 - val_acc: 0.4904
Epoch 3/30
80s - loss: 7.2396 - acc: 0.5029 - val_loss: 7.0901 - val_acc: 0.5024
Epoch 4/30
80s - loss: 2.4306 - acc: 0.5337 - val_loss: 0.6863 - val_acc: 0.5505
Epoch 5/30
80s - loss: 0.7084 - acc: 0.6006 - val_loss: 0.6586 - val_acc: 0.6178
```

References:

Relevant work to MIIL by AIHPC cloud - Azure face emotions:

https://azure.microsoft.com/en-us/services/cognitive-services/emotion/

TRAINING NOTES

36. How to measure the MIIL training effect?

After the AI model machine is trained, the loss and accuracy of using the trained model to classify new test (validation) pictures shall be the metrics to measure the training effect.

```
#4 - Small Conv Net - 3)Evaluating on validation set
evaluate_generator(model,validation_generator, validation_samples)

> evaluate_generator(model,validation_generator, validation_samples)
[[1]]
[1] 1.341891

[[2]]
[1] 0.6887019
```

Here is the training effect by the accuracy metric. The neural network reaches ~69% accuracy. Hence, the implicit image learning through training by the machines has resulted in ~69% accuracy for using the trained AI model to classify new pictures, 19% better than the chance of 50%. The AI machines do not need to specify and reason the complex rules of the trained AI model to achieve the significant MIIL training effect.

References:

@misc{chollet2015keras, title={Keras}, author={Chollet, Fran\c{c}ois and others}, year={2015}, publisher={GitHub}, howpublished={\url{https://github.com/fchollet/keras}},}

Rajiv Shah, https://github.com/rajshah4/image_keras

DeepCyber of Maryland, https://github.com/yeswici/image_keras

TRAINING NOTES

37. Google TSA MIIL competition

To further illustrate the details of MIIL training and computing, we introduce a practical MIIL research and study use case by a Google TSA completion on image machine learning.

Kaggle, a company owned by Google, collaborated with TSA (a federal agency responsible for airport security) to host a competition to predict the probability that a given body zone (out of 17 total body zones) has a threat present. There are more than three terabytes image files that may be analyzed for the predictions.

TRAINING NOTES

38. Real-world MIIL use case: Preparations

The objective of the real-world use-case (nicknamed as *Catch Cats* or *CC* experiment) is to detect threats in scanned TSA images. The *CC* preparations are:

1) Code tsa_read_images.R (under */home/ubuntu/image_keras/R*) to extract the first *a3saps* zip file (*00360f79fd6e02781457eda48f85da90.a3daps*) to PNG images files

2) Transfer the image files to the AIHPC cloud

3) Code *rename,php* (under /home/ubuntu/image_keras/data_tsa) to rename and reorder the image files in the AIHPC cloud

4) Create a new folder *data_tsa* to hold TSA image files in a pre-set folder structure (*threats* in the TSA images are nicknamed as *cats*):

    /home/ubuntu/image_keras/data_tsa   *–> train*   *-> cats*

                                               -> dogs

                              -> validation -> cats

                                               -> dogs

References:

TSA = Transportation Security Administration

TSA image files:

1) https://www.kaggle.com/c/passenger-screening-algorithm-challenge/data

2) https://console.cloud.google.com/storage/browser/kaggle-tsa-stage1/stage1/a3daps/?authuser=0

TRAINING NOTES

39. How to transfer image files to AIHPC cloud?

1) sudo apt-get install vsftpd

2) sudo vi /etc/vsftpd.conf

3) uncomment *#write_enable=YES* to *write_enable=YES*

4) sudo service vsftpd restart

5) WinSCP to connect with AIHPC cloud user *ubuntu*

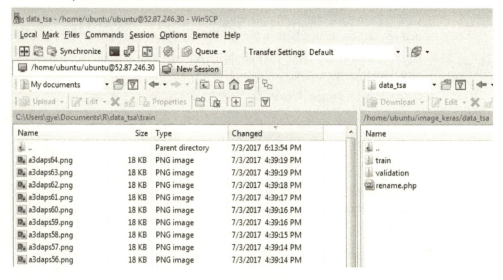

TRAINING NOTES

AIHPC® Cloud

40. TSA MIIL execution and training effect

The R program *tsa_mil.R* (under */home/ubuntu/image_keras/R*) runs neural-network (NN) training and predictions to the TSA image files on the AIHPC cloud.

Using the trained neural-network model to test images in the validation or assessment phase, the result for the first *a3saps* file shows that it is possible to achieve above **97% accuracy** (i.e., the MIIL training effect) in detecting threats from the first set of TSA scanned images. Note that the testing/validation images are the same as the training images. Both come from the first *a3saps* file: *00360f79fd6e02781457eda48f85da90.a3daps*.

```
Epoch 1/30
4s - loss: 0.3269 - acc: 0.9688 - val_loss: 1.0000e-07 - val_acc: 1.0000
Epoch 2/30
3s - loss: 1.0000e-07 - acc: 1.0000 - val_loss: 1.0000e-07 - val_acc: 1.0000
Epoch 3/30
3s - loss: 1.0000e-07 - acc: 1.0000 - val_loss: 1.0000e-07 - val_acc: 1.0000
Epoch 4/30
3s - loss: 1.0745e-07 - acc: 1.0000 - val_loss: 1.0000e-07 - val_acc: 1.0000
Epoch 5/30
3s - loss: 1.0000e-07 - acc: 1.0000 - val_loss: 1.0000e-07 - val_acc: 1.0000
Epoch 6/30
3s - loss: 1.0000e-07 - acc: 1.0000 - val_loss: 1.0000e-07 - val_acc: 1.0000
Epoch 7/30
3s - loss: 1.0000e-07 - acc: 1.0000 - val_loss: 1.0000e-07 - val_acc: 1.0000
```

TRAINING NOTES

41. Testing new TSA images

The objective is to use the images of the second *a3daps* file as validation images to test the trained model from the first *a3daps* file:

The first file = *00360f79fd6e02781457eda48f85da90.a3daps*

The second file = *0043db5e8c819bffc15261b1f1ac5e42.a3daps*

1) download the second *a3daps* file from Google cloud storage

2) upload the second *a3daps* file to the AIHPC cloud

3) extract the *a3daps* file to */home/ubuntu/images* by running *tsa_read_image.R* (under */home/ubuntu/image_keras/R*)

4) rename and add the extracted PNG files (from */home/ubuntu/images*) to */home/ubuntu/image_keras/data_tsa1/validation/cats*

5) run *tsa_mil.R* (under */home/ubuntu/image_keras/R*) for the new test/validation image files

Compared to testing the NN model with the same training images, the accuracy drops to *89%* from *97%* for the first iteration/epoch. The MIIL training effect comes to *100%* after several iterations of fitting the model.

```
> model %>% fit_generator(
+    train_generator,
+    steps_per_epoch = as.integer(train_samples/batch_size),
+    epochs = epochs,
+    validation_data = validation_generator,
+    validation_steps = as.integer(validation_samples/batch_size),
+    verbose=2
+ )
Epoch 1/30
4s - loss: 1.4342 - acc: 0.8906 - val_loss: 1.0000e-07 - val_acc: 1.0000
Epoch 2/30
3s - loss: 1.0000e-07 - acc: 1.0000 - val_loss: 1.0000e-07 - val_acc: 1.0000
Epoch 3/30
3s - loss: 1.0000e-07 - acc: 1.0000 - val_loss: 1.0000e-07 - val_acc: 1.0000
Epoch 4/30

> evaluate_generator(model,validation_generator, validation_samples)
[[1]]
[1] 1e-07

[[2]]
[1] 1
```

42. Deep diving into body zones?

1) Approach 1: 64 images – a single *a3daps* file to produce 64 images per ID of 3D scans

2) Approach 2: 17 zones per image (select from the 64 images) per ID and then aggregate the training/testing metrics by averages.

We think Approach 1 is better than 2 to create a better trained neural-network model for the MIIL experiment with more accuracy. Why?

Approach 1 treats *threats* as a whole in whole body scans. This is in sync with developing an image classifies for cats and dogs that does not split cats/dogs images into pieces or zones.

Approach 2 splits *threats* into pieces (possibly in the 17 body zones). This may mislead the neural-network trainer to develop a less-accurate image classifier because of implement *threat* information per body zone.

TRAINING NOTES

43. Automating file downloads

We may want to consider Approach 2 in a later stage. Yet at first, we implement Approach 1. Instead of detecting pieces of *threats* in 17 body zones of a single image per scan, we train and test 64 images per 3D-scan ID for 17 rounds to collect the accuracy probabilities for each round of training. The implementation steps are:

1) Install Google Cloud SDK

```
https://cloud.google.com/sdk/docs/#deb
gcloud auth application-default login
```

2) Install Google cloud library:

```
sudo apt-get update
sudo apt-get install composer
composer require google/cloud
```

3) Develop and run the main program:

```
Develop tsa_miil_main.php
Run: php tsa_miil_main.php (under ~/tsa)
First, this shall download an a3dasp file programmatically
```

TRAINING NOTES

44. Automating R/PHP code for one a3daps file

The objective of *tsa_miil_main.php* is to connect *tsa_read_image.R, tsa_mil.R, rename.php,* and other programs to automate the steps to process a new *a3daps* file. The output file contains the new *a3daps* file id and the MIIL probability as the accuracy metric of testing/validating the new *a3daps* images.

```
function process_single_id($id)
{
    get_3d_file($id);
    extract_3d_runR($id);
    CopyRenameImageFiles($id);
    run_miil_R($id);
    write_submission($id);
    reset_tsa($id);
}
```

References:

PHP library to access Google cloud storage:

https://github.com/GoogleCloudPlatform/google-cloud-php

TRAINING NOTES

45. How to process all the *a3daps* files?

The objective of the MIIL *CC* project is to produce and report the accuracy probability metrics for all the TSA *a3daps* files.

```
$arr_ids = get_id_list();
function process_all_ids($arr)
{
    for($i=0; $i<=sizeof($arr); $i++)
    {
            process_single_id ($arr[$i]);
    }
}
```

TRAINING NOTES

46. How to run/monitor TSA MIIL on AIHPC EC2?

1) Run TSA MIIL and save screen output to *log*

```
~/tsa$ php tsa_miil_main.php | tee log
```

2) Count number of a3dasp files processed in real-time

```
~/tsa$ grep round_1, stage1_submission.txt |wc
```

3) Check submission output in real-time

```
~/tsa$ tail -f stage1_submission.txt
```

TRAINING NOTES

47. Sample submission output

Below is part of a sample submission with accuracy probability as the prediction metric. Alternatively, loss probability (1 - accuracy) may be used as the prediction metric.

```
1   Id, Accuracy Probability of Aggregated Body Zones for 17 Training Rounds
2   00360f79fd6e02781457eda48f85da90_round_0,0.5625
3   00360f79fd6e02781457eda48f85da90_round_1,1.0000
4   00360f79fd6e02781457eda48f85da90_round_2,1.0000
5   00360f79fd6e02781457eda48f85da90_round_3,1.0000
6   00360f79fd6e02781457eda48f85da90_round_4,1.0000
7   00360f79fd6e02781457eda48f85da90_round_5,1.0000
8   00360f79fd6e02781457eda48f85da90_round_6,1.0000
9   00360f79fd6e02781457eda48f85da90_round_7,1.0000
10  00360f79fd6e02781457eda48f85da90_round_8,0.9844
11  00360f79fd6e02781457eda48f85da90_round_9,1.0000
12  00360f79fd6e02781457eda48f85da90_round_10,1.0000
13  00360f79fd6e02781457eda48f85da90_round_11,1.0000
14  00360f79fd6e02781457eda48f85da90_round_12,1.0000
15  00360f79fd6e02781457eda48f85da90_round_13,1.0000
16  00360f79fd6e02781457eda48f85da90_round_14,1.0000
17  00360f79fd6e02781457eda48f85da90_round_15,1.0000
18  00360f79fd6e02781457eda48f85da90_round_16,1.0000
```

TRAINING NOTES

48.   Machine Memories Framework

Machine memories are part of machine intelligence that resembles human memory, which is part of human intelligence including learning, memory, choice and decision making. Machine memories use AI algorithms and machine learning technologies on top of computer memory and storage to make machines operate as how human memory works.

Due to aging and drug abuse, one's memories may degrade over time. How to restore the memories that are useful yet fading away? Biologists and psychologists suggest brain regions such as Hippocampus (for memory formation and restoration), Barca (for storage of memories of words), and Visual Cortex (for image processing) are relevant to restore useful memories (see MacKay, The Engine of Memory, Scientific American Summer 2017).

We propose that a machine memories framework (MMF) may function similarly or better in some areas than how human memories work. The MMF may use the AIHPC cloud as the machine computing infrastructure: for processing images (as Visual Cortex), the MMF uses the artificial intelligence platforms of AIHPC cloud such as TensorFlow, MXNet, Weka, ImageJ, and OpenCV3; for storing memories (as Barca), the MMF uses SSD and disk storages of AIHPC cloud or its on-premise storage mechanism; for restoring memories (as Hippocampus), the MMF uses the HPC and Big Data computing capabilities of the AIHPC cloud.

TRAINING NOTES

Section 2: SaaS on AIHPC

---

49.   PNN Earnings Cycles (PEC) App for Stocks

AIHPC cloud has served as the backend engines for PNN AI applications. PNN stands for predictive neural nets, which is a trademarked and patented financial AI product for investment management as the first trend-spotting AI machine. PNN helps asset managers rank and optimize portfolios for better returns. See https://yeswici.com for a brief introduction.

PNN Earnings Cycles (PEC) app refers to one of the PNN AI applications that are running on the AIHPC cloud platforms. It builds on the new finding of an AI pattern called PNN Earnings Cycles (PEC): PNN selects a group of stocks that operate responsively to earnings calls in a predictable pattern. As a result, the PEC app has successfully advised actions and no-actions for practical asset management. The plot below shows the returns of the PNN earnings cycles for one of the PNN stocks. For the recent five earnings cycles, the stock returns 4% to 22% per cycle.

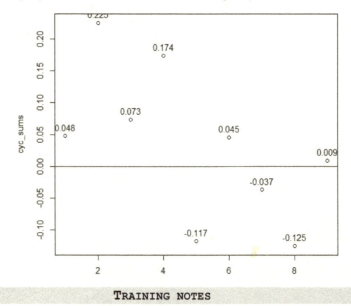

TRAINING NOTES

AIHPC® Cloud

50. PNN Peaks (PP) App for Stocks

When will share prices peak? The PNN Peaks app on the AIHPC cloud computerizes the algorithmic pattern that captures the peak times and values of PNN stocks. The chart below shows the peak times and values in red dots for a PNN stock.

The new AI algorithm of the PP app discovered that the peaks of PNN stocks follow a pattern to appear. Along with the PEC app, this PP pattern has been applied to practical asset risk management to avoid huge investment losses.

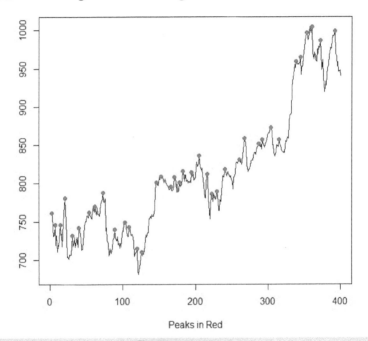

Peaks in Red

TRAINING NOTES

AIHPC® Cloud

51.   PNN Buyback (PBB) App for Stocks

Both AAPL and BABA have established strong shares buyback programs to reward investors. Can the buyback programs also improve its share performance? How to smarten the buyback programs to maximize the share performance over time? We understand that a CEO's performance is primarily assessed by the board and investors on the company's share performance.

The PNN Buyback (PBB) app on AIHPC cloud is designed for CEOs to use PNN Table app (see a sample below) and PNN Earnings Cycles (PEC) app to plan the buyback dates and amounts in order to hold up the desirable trends of share performance.

PNN Table for Asset Managers to Optimize Portfolios/ETF Funds - Trendspotting AI® Nightly Report

Rank	Ticker	cPrice	fAvgTrend	fRisk	Grade	GradeChange	LatestGradeChangeDate
1	AAPL	146.58	30.88%	28.75	★★★★★	No Change	Upgraded on 2017-04-15
2	NKE	54.99	20%	5.31	★★★	Downgraded	Downgraded on 2017-05-02
3	BP	34.32	12.16%	0.94	★★★★	No Change	Upgraded on 2017-04-20
4	TGT	55.77	7.3%	1	★★★	No Change	Downgraded on 2017-04-06
5	XOM	82.06	4.12%	1.26	★★★	No Change	Benchmark Grade on 2017-03-07
6	FB	152.46	-0.92%	0.8	★★★	No Change	Benchmark Grade on 2017-03-07
7	DAL	45.4	-5.05%	0.55	★★★	No Change	Benchmark Grade on 2017-04-05
8	GE	28.99	-6.79%	1.21	★★★	No Change	Upgraded on 2017-05-01
9	GS	224.85	-8.81%	5.94	★★★	No Change	Upgraded on 2017-04-22
10	BAC	23.61	-9.5%	1.28	★★★	No Change	Upgraded on 2017-04-14
11	JNJ	123.34	-15.59%	4.81	★★	No Change	Upgraded on 2017-04-16
12	JPM	87.06	-18%	4.9	★★	No Change	Upgraded on 2017-04-24
13	MS	43.74	-21.17%	2.35	★	No Change	Downgraded on 2017-05-02
14	MSFT	68.46	-21.71%	4	★	No Change	Downgraded on 2017-04-21
15	COST	177.86	-22.29%	9.21	★	No Change	Downgraded on 2017-04-29

Created on 2017-05-02 - Yeswici LLC ©2017. PNN®, MD USA. All Rights Reserved. About PNN AI

TRAINING NOTES

52. How to install Blockchain Bootstrap on AIHPC?

To jumpstart the technical understanding of blockchain concepts, you may follow the steps to install the blockchain bootstrap app on your AIHPC cloud:

1) Launch an AIHPC cloud instance; see Topic 4 - How to launch AIHPC cloud instances.

2) SSH into EC2 console and download the app repo from *yeswici*'s github

```
$ git clone https://github.com/yeswici/blockchain-demo.git
```

3) Go to the app folder and install dependencies

```
$ cd blockchain-demo/
$ sudo apt-get update
$ sudo apt-get install npm
$ sudo apt-get install nodejs
$ sudo ln -s /usr/bin/nodejs /usr/bin/node
$ npm install
```

4) Start the Web server and app

```
$ ./bin/www
```

5) Point a Web browser at the blockchain bootstrap app with this URL

```
http://{IP Address of the AIHPC EC2 Instance}:3000
```

TRAINING NOTES

53.   How to Make Changes to the Blockchain Repo?

You may fork the github repo (https://github.com/yeswici/blockchain-demo) and use it as a code base to develop your own blockchain app on the AIHPC cloud server. To commit the code changes to your own repo, follow the steps:

1) Fork the github repo (https://github.com/yeswici/blockchain-demo)

2) SSH into AIHPC EC2 and download the app repo from {your own repo}

```
$ git clone https://github.com/{your own repo}/blockchain-demo.git
```

3) Make code changes to your local repo copy

4) Add, commit, and push the code changes to your remote (github) repo

$ git add * {enter your github username and password}

```
$ git commit -m "Customized for AIHPC"
$ git push origin master
```

yeswici Customized for AIHPC

bin	initial import
locales	Customized for AIHPC
public	Add donation image
routes	initial import
views	Customized for AIHPC

(Credit goes to Anders Brownworth who created the original github repo)

TRAINING NOTES

54.   Why Build Blockchain Apps on AIHPC Cloud?

First, the blockchain bootstrap app on AIHPC provides a decent foundation for you to build your own blockchain apps with AI and HPC capabilities. Similar to bitcoin and ethereum, your innovative blockchain app could be created if you find a meaningful connection between the blockchain capabilities and the AIHPC capabilities.

Second, running the blockchain bootstrap app on the AIHPC cloud enables the potential for you to stand on giant shoulders to leap forward by bridging the two hottest technologies: blockchain and artificial intelligence.

Third, the blockchain bootstrap app is open sourced thus you may extend the code and the capabilities of the app on the AIHPC cloud. The capabilities of the blockchain bootstrap app on the AIHPC cloud include hash crypto, block, blockchain, distributed blockchain and tokens. Topic 56 to Topic 60 shall elaborate these capabilities.

For example, you may use both the bootstrap app and the AIHPC AI platforms to create new blockchain apps such as 1) securing TensorFlow datasets of the AIHPC platform with SHA-256 hash functions of the blockchain technology; 2) analyzing blockchain transactions (tokens) of bootstrap-powered apps on neural nets with the MXNet platform of the AIHPC cloud.

Blockchain apps are expected to make significant contributions in many industries and businesses including payment, smart contracts, settlement, supply chain, digital identity, voting, healthcare, and insurance contracts, etc. We are developing a new blockchain app with the bootstrap code repo on the AIHPC cloud.

TRAINING NOTES

55.   Famous Blockchain Apps: Bitcoin and Ethereum

Building on the blockchain technology, bitcoin and ethereum have made significant impact to the financial world. Bitcoin is the first digital currency based on the blockchain technology. As of September 4th 2017, the bitcoin unit price has risen 622.99% since last year (see coinbase charts: https://www.coinbase.com/charts).

Ethereum is considered as bitcoin 2.0. It is a prominent next-generation blockchain platform that can issue new digital currency and crowd-sale the new digital currency.

Normally startup companies face challenges to raise funds to create and substantiate novel business models. The ethereum platform offers an automated approach and large audience to connect investors with innovations through new digital currencies.

Similar to IPO (Initial Public Offering) to raise public funds through exchanges, ICO (Initial Coin Offering) may use the ethereum platform to raise funds from the blockchain network,

Bitcoin · $4,388.72   Ethereum · $308.99   Litecoin · $69.87   1H 1D 1W

$4,388.72   +$3,781.70   +622.99%
BITCOIN PRICE   SINCE LAST YEAR (USD)   SINCE LAST YEAR (%)

TRAINING NOTES

56.   Blockchain Capability 1: SHA-256 Hash

SHA-256 Hash is one of the fundamental capabilities of the blockchain bootstrap app on the AIHPC cloud. SHA stands for Secure Hash Algorithm: a set of cryptographic hash functions designed by the United States National Security Agency (NSA). The SHA-2 family consists of six hash functions with hash values of 224, 256, 384 or 512 bits. SHA-256 hash uses the hash function with the hash value of 256 bits.

You may get instant hash values for the data entered in the blockchain app on the AIHPC cloud. Given that you have followed the steps of Topic 52, you may access the page below by clicking the "Hash" link from the home page of the blockchain app on the AIHPC cloud (http://{IP Address of the AIHPC EC2 Instance}:3000). Type some text such as "AIHPC" in the Text box; then the SHA-256 hash value for the text shall show up automatically below the Text box. The hash value is calculated by the nodejs code of the blockchain bootstrap app available in the github repo.

SHA256 Hash

Data: AIHPC

Hash: c1c7321c48e89421deb0fddd06db0f02b9925ddd143a87466a36a34e4a82ff9e

```
function sha256(block, chain) {
  // calculate a SHA256 hash of the contents of the block
  return CryptoJS.SHA256(getText(block, chain));
}
```

TRAINING NOTES

57. Blockchain Capability 2: Block

A block adds two new sections to Data and Hash; block number and Nonce. Block numbers are ordered to label the blocks. Nonces are one time random numbers that may only be used once to build the final hash value. Blocks are building blocks of a blockchain.

Clicking on the "Block" link of the blockchain bootstrap app on the AIHPC cloud would show a block with Block number, Nonce, Data, and Hash sections. You may add or change the values in any of the three sections of Block number, Nonce, and Data. This would turn the background color to *pink* from *green* as the hash value may automatically change to four non-zeros at the beginning. Clicking on the "Mine" button below the Text box would change the hash value to a new one starting with four zeros, followed by the background color changing to *green* from *pink*.

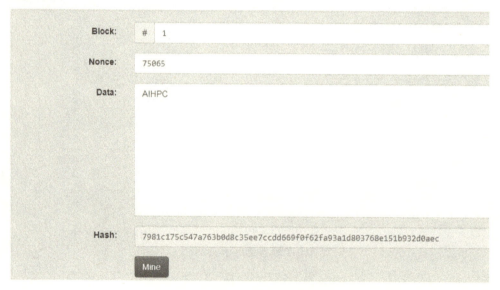

AIHPC® Cloud

58. Blockchain Capability 3: Blockchain

Building on blocks, a blockchain connects multiple blocks. A "Prev" section is added to each of the member blocks to indicate the hash value of previous block that the current block is connected to. Any change to a block section could break the integrity of the blockchain and result in *pink* background for all subsequent blocks. You need to "Mine" the affected blocks of the blockchain to make the background *green* again.

You may access the "Blockchain" page as seen below by clicking the "Blockchain" link of the blockchain bootstrap app on the AIHPC cloud.

Blockchain Bootstrap on AIHPC   Hash   Block   **Blockchain**

Blockchain on AIHPC

Block:	# 1
Nonce:	11316
Data:	
Prev:	0000000000000000000000000000000000000000
Hash:	000015783b764259d382017d91a36d206d0600

Mine

Block:	# 2
Nonce:	35230
Data:	
Prev:	000015783b764259d382017d91a36d206d0600
Hash:	000012fa9b916eb9078f8d98a7864e697ae83e

Mine

TRAINING NOTES

AIHPC® Cloud

---

59. Blockchain Capability 4: Distributed Blockchain

A distributed blockchain is a network of multiple blockchains labeled as Peers. For example, Peer A and Peer B blockchain form a distributed blockchain as shown below. You may access the "Distributed Blockchain" page as seen below by clicking the "Distributed" link of the blockchain bootstrap app on the AIHPC cloud.

Distributed Blockchain

Peer A

Block:	# 1	Block:	# 2
Nonce:	11316	Nonce:	35230
Data:		Data:	
Prev:	0000000000000000000000000000000000000000000000000000000000000000	Prev:	000015783b764259d382017d91a36d206d0600e2cbb3567748f46a33f
Hash:	000015783b764259d382017d91a36d206d0600e2cbb3567748f46a33f	Hash:	000012fa9b916eb9078f8d98a7864e697ae83ed54f5146bd84452cdaf
	Mine		Mine

Peer B

Block:	# 1	Block:	# 2
Nonce:	11316	Nonce:	35230
Data:		Data:	

TRAINING NOTES

---

60. Blockchain Capability 5: Tokens

Tokens make distributed blockchains useful for financial transactions in crypto by extending the "Data" section with all-or-nothing transactions (i.e., from "Data" to "Tx"). The "Tx" section of a block of a token could be filled with records of financial activities.

For example, the first transaction of the "Tx" section of Block #1 of Peer A blockchain records the financial activity of transferring $25 from Darcy to Bingley. You may access the Tokens page as seen below by clicking the "Tokens" link of the blockchain bootstrap app on the AIHPC cloud.

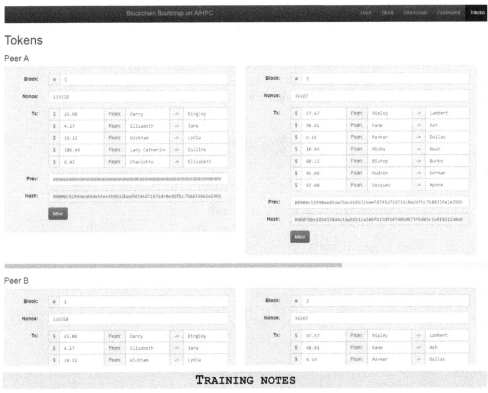

TRAINING NOTES

AIHPC® Cloud

Section 3: Blockchain Security

61.   How to Secure AI Data by Blockchain Hash/Salt?

AI data such as TensorFlow datasets on the AIHPC cloud may be secured by the Hash and Salt function of the blockchain bootstrap app. *Salt* is a random number added to the data for the one-way SHA-256 hashing in order to prevent reverse-hashing such as using rainbow tables to crack the data. Nonce (see the image for Topic 57) is the *Salt* for the blockchain bootstrap app for the AIHPC cloud.

Below are the source code locations on the AIHPC cloud server and the code snippets for constructing and hashing the data plus salt/nonce. A REST API and a console utility to hash the data and salt are also available on the AIHPC cloud.

The API and the console utility form the foundation of the Blockchain Bootstrap Security (BBS) server for the AIHPC GovCloud with the following github repo: https://github.com/yeswici/blockchain-demo.

```
~/blockchain-demo/views $ vi block.jade
function getText(block, chain) {
        return $('#block'+block+'chain'+chain+'number').val() +
        $('#block'+block+'chain'+chain+'nonce').val() +
        $('#block'+block+'chain'+chain+'data').val();
}


~/blockchain-demo/public/javascripts $ vi blockchain.js
function sha256(block, chain) {
        // calculate a SHA256 hash/salt of the contents of the block
        return CryptoJS.SHA256(getText(block, chain));
}


~/blockchain-demo/public/javascripts $ vi www_hashsalt.js
//REST API Usage:
//1 start API REST server: node www_hashsalt.js
//2 web: http://localhost:3001/?data=123&salt=456

~/blockchain-demo/public/javascripts $ vi call_hashsalt_api.js
//Console Usage: node call_hashsalt_api.js "data " salt
```

TRAINING NOTES

62.   Quantum Key Distribution (QKD) – Why

One of the future challenges to blockchain security as SHA-256 hashing and salts is that powerful quantum computers (e.g., the quantum servers of Google cloud platform) may launch successful attacks to the SHA-256 algorithms and salts. Theoretically quantum computers may quickly solve the mathematical algorithms behind the SHA-256 hashes, hence make digital signatures of blocks (prev. hash, see the picture of Topic 58) of block chains insecure (Kiktenko 2017).

One solution to the quantum attacks is implementing post-quantum digital signature schemes (Bernstein 2009) for signing transactions. Yet, it requires too intense computation to be realistic in practice. Another solution is implementing quantum key distribution (QKD) that guarantees the blockchain security from quantum attacks based on the laws of quantum physics (Gisin et al. 2002). The QKD solution has been well respected in practice as being implemented in satellite-to-ground communications with a dedicated satellite called Mozi (Liao et al. 2017).

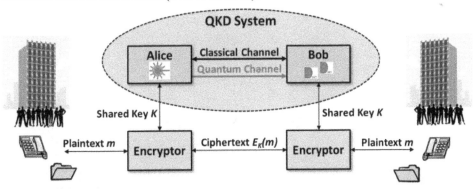

From Cyber Security & Information Systems Information Analysis Center | csiac.org

References:

Kiktenko, E.O. et al (2017), Quantum-secured blockchain, arXiv:1705.09258 [quant-ph]

Bernstein, D.J. Introduction to post-quantum cryptography (Springer-Verlag Berlin Heidelberg, 2009).

Gisin, N., Ribordy, G., Tittel, W., & Zbinden H. (2002) Quantum cryptography. Rev. Mod. Phys. 74, 145 - 195.

Liao, Sheng-Kai et al. (2017), Satellite-to-ground quantum key distribution, Nature, 549(7670):43-47.

63.   QKD Extends BBS on Quantum Key Generation

How to extend the AIHPC BBS cloud server with a QKD technology to build quantum salts (i.e., Nonces in the Topic 57 picture) and hash values to defend quantum attacks? We may implement one of the QKD technologies, quantum key (random number) generation (QKG), to create the ramdom salts or nonces to build the hash values. The salts or nonces generated by the QKD's quantum key generation (QKG) algorithms are the true one-time random numbers. This is because the quantum keys are unhackable by quantum computers as proved by laws of quantum physics (Gisin et al. 2002).

Note that the AIHPC BBS cloud server extended by quantum key/salt generation (QKG) does not provide an end-to-end QKD solution (see the big-picture diagram below). Yet it focuses on the creation of the one-time random numbers as the salts, or the quantum secret keys in the below big picture. Hence, the QKG extension of the BBS server implements only a part of the QKD, i.e., the QKG. In other words, the QKD algorithms extend the BBS server with the QKG implementation.

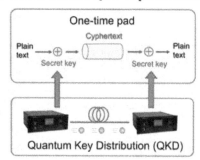

From https://www.nict.go.jp/en/press/2017/07/11-1.html

TRAINING NOTES

64.   AIHPC BBS QKG Solution to Quantum Attacks

We extend the BBS server by implementing our own QKG solution. The next release of AIHPC cloud (https://aws.amazon.com/marketplace/pp/B01JJ31R8C) shall include the native quantum and blockchain security features. The native BBS QKG capability may be used by end users as follows:

For native BBS QKG utilities, a nodejs API was developed to generate quantum keys and enable HTTP(S)-based RESTful access to the salts from an AIHPC cloud. Here is a sample usage (on p24 - a pilot BBS server):

```
$ cd ~/blockchain-demo/public/javascripts

Step 1 - generate a quantum key

$ node get_qsalt.js 5 50

Step 2 - replace salt with the quantum key and run console utility to produce the
quantum hash value

$ node call_hashsalt_api.js "data " salt

Step 3 - replace salt with the quantum key generated and run Web utility to produce
the quantum hash value

$ node www_hashsalt.js
{http://localhost:3001/?data=123&salt=QuantumKey}
```

For native QKG utilities (https://github.com/yeswici/quantumrandom): the quantum keys may be generated by these commands:

```
sudo pip install quantumrandom

$ qrandom --int --min 5 --max 15

$ qrandom --hex

$ qrandom --binary | dd of=data
```

TRAINING NOTES

65.　IDQ Implementation of Quantum Key Generation

There are business, scientific, and national-security markets for buying QKG software. One of the competitors to AIHPC BBS QKG is ID Quantique (IDQ) that was established in Geneva, Switzerland in 2001 by the scientists from the University of Geneva, who anticipated the important forthcoming impact of quantum physics on information technology.

One of IDQ's software is Quantis, a family of hardware random number generators (RNG) or quantum key generation (QKG) solutions. The details about IDG's QKG may be found at http://www.idquantique.com/quantum-safe-crypto/quantum-key-generation.

The differences between BBS QKG and IDQ QKG are (1) BBS OKG is part of AIHPC cloud, thus leading IDQ QKG in cloud solutions as IDQ QKG is not cloud ready; (2) BBS OKG has been implemeted to bootstrap blockchain security while IDG OKG is not blockchain ready; (3) BBS OKG may interact with AI platforms natively in the AIHPC cloud, while IDG OKG does not work with AI machine learning technologies.

TRAINING NOTES

AIHPC® Cloud

Section 4: Blockchain Labs

66.   What is behind Bitcoin Mining?

Bitcoin is a payment token (see Topic 60) secured by blockchain hash and salt (Topic 61). For the blockchain bootstrap app on the AIHPC cloud, bitcoin mining is the sequence of operations to discover new hash values for any *Tx* data that are changed in the chain of blocks.

This bitcoin mining is behind the bitcoin mining businesses in which special bitcoin mining hardware (e.g., AntMiner and Avalon units) are engaged to find new hash values. Cloud mining such as those offered by Hashflare is an alternative to the on-premise mining with the special mining hardware. Regardless of the types of bitcoin mining businesses, the core of the operations is similar to what happens after clicking the *Mine* button of the blockchain bootstrap app for the AIHPC cloud.

Below is the code snippet for the algorithm to mine a payment token and the location of the code file in the AIHPC cloud server. It shows the process to fix the blocks of the chain with new hash values (starting from four zeros) after clicking the *Mine* button.

```
~/blockchain-demo/public/javascripts $ vi blockchain.js
function mine(block, chain, isChain) {
  for (var x = 0; x <= 500000; x++) {
    $('#block'+block+'chain'+chain+'nonce').val(x);
    $('#block'+block+'chain'+chain+'hash').val(sha256(block, chain));
    if ($('#block'+block+'chain'+chain+'hash').val().substr(0, 4) === '0000') {
      if (isChain) {
        updateChain(block, chain);
      }
      else {
        updateState(block, chain);
      }
      break;
    }
  }
}
```

TRAINING NOTES

67.   Configure Apache as a Reverse Proxy

https://devops.profitbricks.com/tutorials/configure-apache-as-a-reverse-proxy-using-mod_proxy-on-ubuntu/

Requirements

A server running Ubuntu-14.04

A static IP Address for your server

Install Apache

Let's start making sure that your Ubuntu-14.04 server is fully up to date. You can update your server by running the following command:

```
sudo apt-get update -y
sudo apt-get upgrade -y
```

With the server up to date, you can continue the process and install Apache on your server. You can install Apache by simply running the following command:

```
sudo apt-get install apache2 -y
```

Once Apache has been installed, start the Apache service and configure it to start automatically when the server boots:

```
sudo /etc/init.d/apache2 start
sudo update-rc.d apache2 defaults
```

Install mod_proxy and other modules

mod_proxy is the Apache module that implements a proxy/gateway for Apache HTTP Server, supporting a number of popular protocols as well as several different load balancing algorithms. It is used to manage connections and redirect them.

You can install mod_proxy and its dependencies using the following command:

```
sudo apt-get install libapache2-mod-proxy-html libxml2-dev -y
```

Let's continue with installing the build-essential package for application building. This package can be used to install certain things from source.

Run the following command to install build-essential package:

```
sudo apt-get install -y build-essential
```

Configure Apache for Proxy

Before configuring Apache, you will need to enable some necessary modules.

Run the following command to get a list of available Apache modules:

```
sudo a2enmod
```

You should see the list of all the modules:

```
Your choices are: access_compat actions alias allowmethods asis auth_basic
auth_digest auth_form authn_anon authn_core authn_dbd authn_dbm authn_file
authn_socache authnz_ldap authz_core authz_dbd authz_dbm authz_groupfile authz_host
authz_owner authz_user autoindex buffer cache cache_disk cache_socache cgi cgid
charset_lite data dav dav_fs dav_lock dbd deflate dialup dir dump_io echo env expires
ext_filter file_cache filter headers heartbeat heartmonitor include info
lbmethod_bybusyness lbmethod_byrequests lbmethod_bytraffic lbmethod_heartbeat ldap
log_debug log_forensic lua macro mime mime_magic mpm_event mpm_prefork mpm_worker
negotiation php5 proxy proxy_ajp proxy_balancer proxy_connect proxy_express
proxy_fcgi proxy_fdpass proxy_ftp proxy_html proxy_http proxy_scgi proxy_wstunnel
ratelimit reflector remoteip reqtimeout request rewrite sed session session_cookie
session_crypto session_dbd setenvif slotmem_plain slotmem_shm socache_dbm
socache_memcache socache_shmcb speling ssl status substitute suexec unique_id userdir
usertrack vhost_alias xml2enc
```

AIHPC® Cloud

```
Which module(s) do you want to enable (wildcards ok)?
```
Next, you can run the following commands to enable the modules one by one:
```
sudo a2enmod proxy
sudo a2enmod proxy_http
sudo a2enmod proxy_ajp
sudo a2enmod rewrite
sudo a2enmod deflate
sudo a2enmod headers
sudo a2enmod proxy_balancer
sudo a2enmod proxy_connect
sudo a2enmod proxy_html
```
Next, you will need to disable Apache default configuration file `000-default.conf` and create a new virtual host file inside the `/etc/apache2/sites-available` directory to set up "proxying" functionality.

To disable the `000-default` file, run:
```
sudo a2dissite 000-default
```
Then, create a new virtual host file:
```
sudo nano /etc/apache2/sites-available/proxy-host
```
Add the following lines to suit your needs:
```
<VirtualHost *:80>
    ServerAdmin webmaster@localhost
    DocumentRoot /var/www/
    ErrorLog ${APACHE_LOG_DIR}/error.log
    CustomLog ${APACHE_LOG_DIR}/access.log combined
    ProxyPreserveHost On
    # Servers to proxy the connection, or
    # List of application servers Usage
    ProxyPass / http://server-ip-address:8080/
    ProxyPassReverse / http://server-ip-address:8080/
    ServerName localhost
</VirtualHost>
```
Save and close the file.

Enable new virtual host file:
```
sudo a2ensite proxy-host
```
You will also need to tell Apache to listen on port **8080**.

You can do this by editing the `ports.conf` file:
```
sudo nano /etc/apache2/ports.conf
```
Add the following line:
```
Listen 8080
```
Save the file and restart Apache.
```
sudo /etc/init.d/apache2 restart
```
Proxying should be working for you now. When you access the URL `http://server-ip-address:80` in a browser, it will show the application which is running on `http://server-ip-address:8080`. The browser is not aware that the application is running on port 8080.

Enable SSL Reverse-Proxy Support

If you want to enable SSL support to your Reverse-Proxy connections, then you will need to enable the SSL module first.

To enable this module, run:
```
sudo a2enmod ssl
```

AIHPC® Cloud

After you have enabled SSL, you'll have to restart the Apache service for the change to be recognized.

```
sudo /etc/init.d/apache2 restart
```

Next, you will need to generate self-signed certificate. For testing purposes, you will need to generate a private key (ca.key) with 2048 bit encryption.

To do this, run:

```
sudo openssl genrsa -out ca.key 2048
```

Then generate a certificate signing request (ca.csr) using the following command:

```
sudo openssl req -nodes -new -key ca.key -out ca.csr
```

You should see the following output:

```
You are about to be asked to enter information that will be incorporated
into your certificate request.
What you are about to enter is what is called a Distinguished Name or a DN.
There are quite a few fields but you can leave some blank
For some fields there will be a default value,
If you enter '.', the field will be left blank.
-----
Country Name (2 letter code) [AU]:IN
State or Province Name (full name) [Some-State]:GUJARAT
Locality Name (eg, city) []:AHMEDABAD
Organization Name (eg, company) [Internet Widgits Pty Ltd]:ITC
Organizational Unit Name (eg, section) []:IT
Common Name (e.g. server FQDN or YOUR name) []:HITESH JETHVA
Email Address []:

Please enter the following 'extra' attributes
to be sent with your certificate request
A challenge password []:
An optional company name []:
```

Lastly, generate a self-signed certificate (ca.crt) of X509 type valid for 365 keys.

```
sudo openssl x509 -req -days 365 -in ca.csr -signkey ca.key -out ca.crt
```

Create a directory to place the certificate files we have created.

```
sudo mkdir /etc/apache2/ssl
```

Next, copy all certificate files to the /etc/apache2/ssl directory.

```
sudo cp ca.crt ca.key ca.csr /etc/apache2/ssl/
```

Now all the certificates are ready. The next thing to do is to set up the Apache to display the new certificate.

For this, you need to create new virtual host file proxy-ssl-host.conf

```
nano /etc/apache2/sites-available/proxy-ssl-host.conf
```

Add the following content:

```
<VirtualHost *:443>
        ServerAdmin webmaster@localhost
        DocumentRoot /var/www/
        ErrorLog ${APACHE_LOG_DIR}/error.log
        CustomLog ${APACHE_LOG_DIR}/access.log combined
        SSLEngine On
        # Set the path to SSL certificate
        # Usage: SSLCertificateFile /path/to/cert.pem
        SSLCertificateFile /etc/apache2/ssl/ca.crt
        SSLCertificateKeyFile /etc/apache2/ssl/ca.key
        ProxyPreserveHost On
        ProxyPass /var/www/ http://server-ip-address:8080/
```

```
        ProxyPassReverse /var/www/ http://server-ip-address:8080/
        ServerName localhost
</VirtualHost>
```

Save and close the file.

Enable new virtual host file:

```
sudo a2ensite proxy-ssl-host.conf
```

Now, restart the Apache service to make this change take effect:

```
sudo /etc/init.d/apache2 restart
```

That's it. You can now access your server using the URL `https://server-ip-address`.

TRAINING NOTES

68.   Why New Cryptocurrencies as AIPD Coins?

Ethereum, some claim as bitcoin 2.0, allows new cryptocurrencies to be created such as Kodakcoin, AIPDcoin and Hcoin. As a revolutionary transformation of its business model, Kodakcoin allows photographers to receive payment for licensing their work immediately in cryptocurrency form.

On January 10th 2018, the stock market applauded the Kodakcoin announcement by doubling the share price of Easten Kodak Company (NYSE: KODK). Similarly, AIPDcoin and Hcoin allow human doctors, working with the AIPD robot doctor, to receive payment for telemedicine work immediately in cryptocurrency form.

What is AIPD? AIPD® runs the next-gen **telemedicine** delivery model on AI and NLP technologies (https://deepcybe.com) and the next-gen business model on cryptocurrency (AIPDcoin and Hcoin).

Only a small percentage of our population (e.g., the rich and power) can afford dedicated personal human doctors hence live healthier and longer. Healthcare inequality is a fundamental challenge to our society. Social and policy solutions such as ObamaCare are difficult to implement. Let's change the world with innovative technology solutions.

We design and implement AI innovations to get everyone a data-driven AI personal doctor (AIPD®) {pronounced /ād/, like "aid" }, i.e., the robot doctor. Go to https://deepcybe.com to have a conversation with the AIPD Robot Doctor.

TRAINING NOTES

69.   How to Get Test ETH from Rinkeby for AIPDcoin?

1. Get the ethereum address for the MetaMask wallet extension and the new contract:
   0x502bedb280a29957aa666b539231400d2495bfc6

2. Post the ether address in Google+ and get the Google+ URL

   https://plus.google.com/u/0/100151624817439396503/posts/BeUigSC62Rn

3. Get test ether from Rinkeby Faucet by entering the Post url at https://faucet.rinkeby.io

4. The AIPDCoin Wallet in MetaMask will show the test ethers

5. Use the test ethers to deploy and launch the AIPD ICO from CoinCreator.

AIHPC® Cloud

70.   How to Deploy and Launch AIPDcoin ICO?

1. Go to https://coinlaunch.market/coincreator/
2. Click Contract
3. Click Deploy and Start ICO

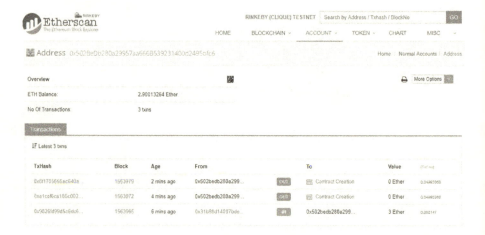

AIHPC® Cloud

71.   After hitting START ICO for Rinkeby?

These steps will happen after hitting START ICO:

Blockchain process

Compiling contracts: ✔

Deploying Crowdsale contract: ✔

Waiting for a mined block to include your contract. ✔

Crowdsale contract has been deployed here. ✔

Deploying Token contract: ✔

Waiting for a mined block to include your contract. ✔

Token contract has been deployed : here. ✔

Updating token contract address in ICO contract and initializing vesting: ✔

Token contract address in ICO contract has been updated and vesting initialized: ✔

Processing Done. ✔

From Rinkeby EtherScan, we find the ICO contract address for the token holder/owner:

https://rinkeby.etherscan.io/token/0x324e7b9aea779f5aec4744d9c74852aab653ab08?a=0x502bedb280a29957aa666b539231400d2495bfc6

Contract Address: 0x324e7b9aea779f5aec4744d9c74852aab653ab08

Token Holder: 0x502bedb280a29957aa666b539231400d2495bfc6

AIHPC® Cloud

72. How to Show Ownership of AIPDcoin?

Below shows the ownership of AIPDCoin in the Rinkeby test network

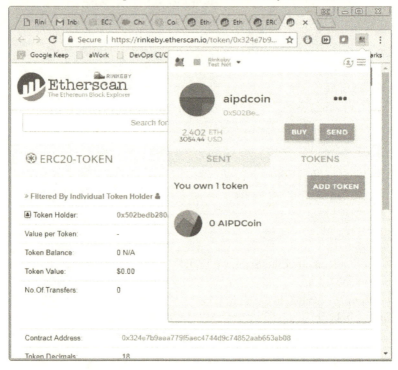

73.   How to Use Geth to Check ETH Balances?

1. Install geth on AIHPC AWS EC2 (DeepCyber Regular AWS US N. VA Region)

```
$ cd /home/ubuntu/eth
$ sudo apt-get install software-properties-common
$ sudo add-apt-repository -y ppa:ethereum/ethereum
$ sudo apt-get update
$ sudo apt-get install ethereum
```

2. Geth to start node and mining or connect to Rinkeby network

- ./mine.sh
- geth --rinkeby --syncmode "fast"

3. Check account balances from another terminal

- geth attach
- > loadScript('check.js')
- > checkAllBalances()
  ```
  0x1cd37d96b33f9ad2f232e9f280305295025ce46a:    balance: 0 ether
  0x652b81f15f3e133077e632b3853b7fffd3e10ae7:    balance: 0 ether
  0x502bedb280a29957aa666b539231400d2495bfc6:    balance: 0 ether
  ```

TRAINING NOTES

AIHPC® Cloud

74.   Create a Private AIPD Net and Mine ETHs

Start and SSH into AWS AIHPC EC2 instance, then

- cd /home/ubuntu/eth/aipd
- cat CustomGenesis.json
- ./g1.sh {start initial private chain}
- ./g2.sh {mine new blocks and add to the private chain}
- ./attach.sh {in another terminal, run this after ./g2.sh to get a JS console}

```
ps aux | less
```

The AIPD private network id is 20000616, configured in CustomGenesis.json. In geth JS console for the AIPD private blockchain, create a new account and mine ETHs

- >personal.newAccount()
- eth.coinbase
  "0x30bef62a6e9170f95b1dcb05659e133f85ce63a5"
- >eth.getBalance("0x30bef62a6e9170f95b1dcb05659e133f85ce63a5")
- >miner.start()
- > eth.getBalance("0x30bef62a6e9170f95b1dcb05659e133f85ce63a5")
  280000000000000000000000
- >miner.stop()
- >loadScript('check.js')
- >checkAllBalances()
  0x30bef62a6e9170f95b1dcb05659e133f85ce63a5:   balance: 1510 ether

AIHPC® Cloud

75. Users Connect to the AIPD Net and Mine ETHs

Get to an Ubuntu Linux, preferably AIHPC EC2 instance.

To run a light node, download `aipd.json` and start `geth` on the `Ubuntu server` with:

- `geth --datadir=$HOME/.aipd init aipd.json`
- `geth --networkid=2000616 --datadir=$HOME/.aipd --syncmode=light --bootnodes=enode://a24ac7c5484ef4ed0c5eb2d36620ba4e4aa13b8c84684e1b4aab0cebe a2ae45cb4d375b77eab56516d34bfbd3c1a833fc51296ff084b770b94fb9028c4d25ccf@52. 169.42.101:30303?discport=30304`

AIHPC® Cloud

76.   Set Up Development Environment with Truffle

On AIHPC EC2 Server, install testrpc

- cd ~/eth/aipd
- sudo apt-get update
- sudo apt install curl
- curl -sL https://deb.nodesource.com/setup_6.x | sudo bash -
- sudo apt-get install -y nodejs
- sudo apt-get install npm
- sudo apt-get install git
- sudo npm install -g ethereumjs-testrp
- testrpc

Create a new nodejs project using Web3 in a separate terminal with testrpc running

- mkdir dapp && cd dapp
- vi package.json
- npm install
- node
- > var Web3 = require("web3")
- > var web3 = new Web3(new
  Web3.providers.HttpProvider("http://localhost:8545"))
- > web3.eth.accounts

Install truffle and create a new project in /home/ubuntu/eth/aipd/dapp/

- sudo npm install -g truffle
- mkdir proj && cd proj
- truffle init
- truffle console
- >web3.eth.accounts
- truffle compile
- truffle migrate

Details at https://www.codeooze.com/blockchain/ethereum-dev-environment/

77. Deploy AIPDcoin Contract and Truffle

```
$ cd /home/ubuntu/eth/aipd/dapp {in terminal 1}
$ mkdir proj
$ cd proj
$ truffle init
$ cd contracts
$ vi aipd.sol
$ vi ../migrations/2_deploy_contracts.js
$ testrpc   {in terminal 2}
$ truffle compile {in terminal 1}
$ truffle migrate {deploy aipd contract to testrpc}
$ truffle console {interact with the contract on the blockchain}
> web3.eth.accounts
> var ac1 = web3.eth.accounts[0]
> var ac2 = web3.eth.accounts[1]
> var app
> aipd.deployed().then(function(instance) { app = instance; })
> app.creator.call()
> app.message.call()
```

Detail at https://www.codeooze.com/blockchain/ethereum-truffle-hello-world

TRAINING NOTES

78.　　Create AIPDcoin Contract Code by Solidity

```
$ cd /home/ubuntu/eth/aipd/dapp/proj
$vi contracts/aipd.sol
pragma solidity ^0.4.0;
contract aipd {
    address public creator; // data-type 'address'
    uint public myNumber; // data-type 'unit'
    string public message; // data-type 'string'

    // constructor - runs once on contract creation transaction
    function aipd() {
        // set 'creator' variable to address of transaction sender
        creator = msg.sender;
        message = 'Hello, aipd'; // set our message
        myNumber = 5; // also set a number
    }
}

$ vi migrations/2_deploy_contracts.js
//var ConvertLib = artifacts.require("./ConvertLib.sol");
//var MetaCoin = artifacts.require("./MetaCoin.sol");
var aipd = artifacts.require("./HelloWorld.sol");

module.exports = function(deployer) {
  //deployer.deploy(ConvertLib);
  //deployer.link(ConvertLib, MetaCoin);
  //deployer.deploy(MetaCoin);
  deployer.deploy(aipd);
};

$ cd /home/ubuntu/eth/aipd/dapp/proj
$ vi truffle.js
module.exports = {
   networks: {
   development: {
   host: "localhost",
   port: 8545,
   network_id: "*" // Match any network id
  }
 }
};
```

More at https://www.codeooze.com/blockchain/ethereum-geth-private-blockchain/

AIHPC® Cloud

79. Develop AIPDcoin and Hcoin Contracts in Remix

https://ethereum.github.io/browser-solidity/#optimize=false&version=soljson-v0.4.19+commit.c4cbbb05.js

≪ ± browser/aipdcoin.sol ✕

```
1  pragma solidity ^0.4.0;
2  contract Ballot {
3
4      struct Voter {
5          uint weight;
6          bool voted;
7          uint8 vote;
8          address delegate;
9      }
10     struct Proposal {
11         uint voteCount;
12     }
13
14     address chairperson;
15     mapping(address => Voter) voters;
16     Proposal[] proposals;
17
18     /// Create a new ballot with $(_numProposals) different proposals.
19     function Ballot(uint8 _numProposals) public {
20         chairperson = msg.sender;
21         voters[chairperson].weight = 1;
22         proposals.length = _numProposals;
23     }
```

TRAINING NOTES

AIHPC® Cloud

80.　　Add AIPD Net in MetaMask

1. Open Port 8545 in AWS Security Group (e,g, dc2) for the AIHPC EC2 server.

2. On AIHPC EC2 whose IP address is 34.227.110.70

   ```
   $ cd /home/ubuntu/eth/aipd
   $ testrpc
   ```

3. Add AIPD Network to MetaMask Wallet: MegaMast Wallte Chrom extension -> Setting -> New RPC -> Add http://34.227.110.70:8545

4. Add and connect to the AIPD private network

81. Add Hcoin accounts to MetaMask

1. Run $s_testrpc.sh and get the private keys for Hcoin accounts

```
$ cd /home/ubuntu/eth/aipd/dapp/proj
$ ./ s_testrpc_persistaccounts.sh
{testrpc --db /home/ubuntu/eth/aipd/dapp/proj/db -d}
Available Accounts
==================
(0) 0xc485677f00d13c8a6ed424a4a5e137b87c812cbd
(1) 0x833cb9657c32d580cabf2b3b76f6824cb8398ebd
(2) 0x0dcfebdaf77dd2800cbd6ec3c827ad40bc742c8f
(3) 0xb3f746aa67f389ba028cb7c7b7cbb7abecb30cbd
(4) 0x7edfb868a17e933c334a83cceb584d89827651ad
(5) 0x92ab634edb291c9f4abf1045e2f533b2505987bc
(6) 0xc7cd708f8a8598b887b24de36db0143dca35bac9
(7) 0x54c41b5f0c95a584242924f98d9e2aba5ce3bb56
(8) 0x2a251490c0be0767291c5b8742c4fc6c3d94e50d
(9) 0xfdab26b1c018e3427bb2d8732d4fb4977ac71eb9

Private Keys
==================
(0) 7dd95c04b58c779f06a625981fd06197909a2ae942c71dd8569fc7108d6a9c9c
(1) 993f698ecf1a0783c0ebe0db97e0ed9e45dc49a97c0e66d2c182197e2b14bd6c
(2) 4c170034f1c14caf657b6b6a4734ab49612e3117350b1f1ca1e9b68ab85dd739
(3) 082cae55ffd05a91bf205ebe3db4083bdfb31df8247999155a5cf19f0b4d1998
(4) 9f97048fdb5d766b230ba0f4001529ff414dfd5ee0c3e25417a22c6577ded8a3
(5) be622976dc8d04a52045fbd2fdca69690bbbfb79c7c2db723bbb44f626da846b
(6) f0e074a243164954e03fbc081eee234a390c140128938af28cd0df74abed957c
(7) 2e973f4b44589540e6cce19b77629ea2e585623f5235453330fce4ccdec4a301
(8) 79e185d50a09c0cbe1d173402e1bc3144e87da537e06df9a7173d901c26de85d
(9) 28d880bdd393762bb921ef735ad91ea1476d3f00f7a4ef0e7a3a54f57c3f177f
```

2. Import a Hcoin account of the private AIPD net to MetaMask

AIHPC® Cloud

82. How to Send ETHs in AIDP Net?

Send ETHs from the private AIPD network to MetaMask Wallet,

- $cd /home/ubuntu/eth/aipd
- $cat CustomGenesis.json
- $./g1.sh {start initial private chain}
- $./g2.sh {mine new blocks and add to the private chain}
- $./attach.sh
- > loadScript("check.js")
- > checkAllBalances()
  0x30bef62a6e9170f95b1dcb05659e133f85ce63a5:   balance: **67385** ether
- > eth.sendTransaction({from: 0x30bef62a6e9170f95b1dcb05659e133f85ce63a5,
  to:0x48d19f6d2702c96f61b9ec20bf3138722c38f3e2, value: 1})

TRAINING NOTES

83.   Import Hcoin Accounts to MetaMask Wallet

1. Get the json key for AIPD net from AIHPC EC2

/home/ubuntu/eth/aipd/ACPrivateChain/keystore

2. Locate MetaMask extention URL on Chrome

chrome-extension://nkbihfbeogaeaoehlefnkodbefgpgknn/popup.html

3. Import the json key file

84.   Get the Balance of Hcoin/MetaMask Accounts

MetaMask can show the balances of the ten default testrpc accounts, each account has 100 ETHs to start.

The balances of the default accounts can be found in truffle console

```
$ testrpc {Terminal 1}
$ truffle console {Terminal 2}

truffle(development)> var balance = (acct) => { return
web3.fromWei(web3.eth.getBalance(acct), 'ether').toNumber()}

truffle(development)> acct1 = web3.eth.accounts[0]
'0x48d19f6d2702c96f61b9ec20bf3138722c38f3e2'

truffle(development)> balance(acct1)
147.99979
```

The same balance, 147.99979, is shown in the MetaMask wallet

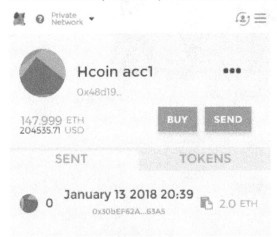

Details at http://truffleframework.com/tutorials/truffle-and-metamask

AIHPC® Cloud

85. Send ETHs between MetaMask Hcoin Accounts

Locate MeteMask Wallet on a dedicated page using URL:

chrome-extension://nkbihfbeogaeaoehlefnkodbefgpgknn/popup.html

AIHPC® Cloud

86. Increase the Balances of Hcoin Accounts

https://github.com/trufflesuite/ganache-cli/blob/master/README.md

ganache-cli replaces and extends testrpc

```
$sudo npm install -g ganache-cli
ganache-cli -p 8555
```

- **Address** = 0x198E13017D2333712Bd942d8B028610b95C363da
- **Private Key** = 7231a774a538fce22a329729b03087de4cb4a1119494db1c10eae3bb491823e7

Start testrpc and specify the account you want to use and the initial balance (**in WEI** 1 ether = 1000000000000000000 wei)

Add 0x before the private key

```
testrpc --account="0x7231a774a538fce22a329729b03087de4cb4a1119494db1c10eae3bb491823e7,
10000000000000000000000"
```

87. Persist Hcoin Accounts after Restarting TestRPC

```
/ubuntu/home//eth/aipd/dapp/proj$ ./s_testrpc.sh

testrpc --db /home/ubuntu/eth/aipd/dapp/proj/db -d
```

TRAINING NOTES

88.   Truffle Works with TestRPC, Not ganache-cli

```
ubuntu@ip-172-31-52-220:~/eth/aipd/dapp/proj$ vi truffle.js {port is 8545 for testrpc}
ubuntu@ip-172-31-52-220:~/eth/aipd/dapp/proj$ truffle console
truffle(development)>
undefined
truffle(development)>
undefined
truffle(development)> var balance = (acct) => { return
web3.fromWei(web3.eth.getBalance(acct), 'ether').toNumber()}
undefined
truffle(development)> acct1 = web3.eth.accounts[0]
'0x2187697d4ce18b313eaf8a880cb62dccad5f3039'
truffle(development)> balance(acct1)
100
truffle(development)> acct2 = web3.eth.accounts[1]
'0xa78985289a566c87e4b01fe418c0e3d4e872eaad'
truffle(development)> balance(acct2)
100
```

TRAINING NOTES

89.   Use geth to Check Hcoin Account Balances

Normally `get attach` of `attach.sh` {~/eth/aipd of AIHPC EC2} would hit port 30303 of aipd network. In addition, `geth attach` can hit port 8545 on TestRPC.

```
ubuntu@ip-172-31-52-220:~/eth/aipd$ geth attach http://localhost:8545
```

Hence, we run geth commands to check balances of Hcoin accounts

```
$ geth attach http://localhost:8545
> loadScript("check.js")
true
> checkAllBalances()
0xc485677f00d13c8a6ed424a4a5e137b87c812cbd:    balance: 100 ether
0x833cb9657c32d580cabf2b3b76f6824cb8398ebd:    balance: 100 ether
0x0dcfebdaf77dd2800cbd6ec3c827ad40bc742c8f:    balance: 100 ether
0xb3f746aa67f389ba028cb7c7b7cbb7abecb30cbd:    balance: 100 ether
0x7edfb868a17e933c334a83cceb584d89827651ad:    balance: 100 ether
0x92ab634edb291c9f4abf1045e2f533b2505987bc:    balance: 100 ether
0xc7cd708f8a8598b887b24de36db0143dca35bac9:    balance: 100 ether
0x54c41b5f0c95a584242924f98d9e2aba5ce3bb56:    balance: 100 ether
0x2a251490c0be0767291c5b8742c4fc6c3d94e50d:    balance: 100 ether
0xfdab26b1c018e3427bb2d8732d4fb4977ac71eb9:    balance: 100 ether
```

This is similar to using `truffle console` {~/eth/aipd/dapp/proj} to check balances:

```
truffle(development)> ubuntu@ip-172-31-52-220:~/eth/aipd/dapp/proj$ truffle console
truffle(development)> var balance = (acct) => { return
web3.fromWei(web3.eth.getBalance(acct), 'ether').toNumber()}
undefined
truffle(development)> acct7 = web3.eth.accounts[7]
'0x54c41b5f0c95a584242924f98d9e2aba5ce3bb56'
truffle(development)> balance(acct7)
100
```

TRAINING NOTES

AIHPC® Cloud

90. Transfer ETHs between Hcoin Accounts

```
$ geth attach http://localhost:8545
> loadScript("check.js")
> web3.eth.getBalance(web3.eth.coinbase)
100000000000000000000
> web3.eth.sendTransaction({from: web3.eth.coinbase, to:
'0x833cb9657c32d580cabf2b3b76f6824cb8398ebd', value: web3.toWei("0.1", "ether")});
"0x5200efc16e48e32ba4554ca6c63676b0a05d6d34e7af6245a9e2ee29df548273"
> checkAllBalances()
0xc485677f00d13c8a6ed424a4a5e137b87c812cbd:     balance: 99.899999999999979 ether
0x833cb9657c32d580cabf2b3b76f6824cb8398ebd:     balance: 100.1 ether
0x0dcfebdaf77dd2800cbd6ec3c827ad40bc742c8f:     balance: 100 ether
0xb3f746aa67f389ba028cb7c7b7cbb7abecb30cbd:     balance: 100 ether
0x7edfb868a17e933c334a83cceb584d89827651ad:     balance: 100 ether
0x92ab634edb291c9f4abf1045e2f533b2505987bc:     balance: 100 ether
0xc7cd708f8a8598b887b24de36db0143dca35bac9:     balance: 100 ether
0x54c41b5f0c95a584242924f98d9e2aba5ce3bb56:     balance: 100 ether
0x2a251490c0be0767291c5b8742c4fc6c3d94e50d:     balance: 100 ether
0xfdab26b1c018e3427bb2d8732d4fb4977ac71eb9:     balance: 100 ether
```

Reflected in MetaMask Wallet for the two Hcoin accounts

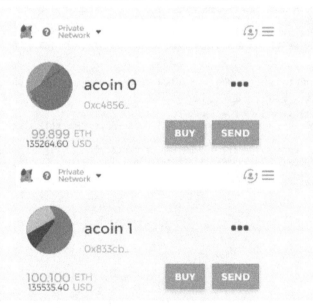

AIHPC® Cloud

91.   Mining ETHs in the Main Ethereum Network

```
ubuntu@ip-172-31-52-220:~/eth/aipd$ geth {Terminal 1}
INFO [01-14|04:56:43] Initialised chain configuration config="{ChainID: 1 Homestead:
1150000 DAO: 1920000 DAOSupport: true EIP150: 2463000 EIP155: 2675000 EIP158: 2675000
Byzantium: 4370000 Engine: ethash}"

ubuntu@ip-172-31-52-220:~/eth/aipd$ geth attach {Terminal 2}
Welcome to the Geth JavaScript console!
instance: Geth/v1.7.3-stable-4bb3c89d/linux-amd64/go1.9
coinbase: 0x1cd37d96b33f9ad2f232e9f280305295025ce46a
at block: 0 (Thu, 01 Jan 1970 00:00:00 UTC)
 datadir: /home/ubuntu/.ethereum
 modules: admin:1.0 debug:1.0 eth:1.0 miner:1.0 net:1.0 personal:1.0 rpc:1.0
txpool:1.0 web3:1.0
> loadScript("check.js")
true
> miner.start()
> checkAllBalances()
0x1cd37d96b33f9ad2f232e9f280305295025ce46a:        balance: 0 ether
0x652b81f15f3e133077e632b3853b7fffd3e10ae7:        balance: 0 ether
0x502bedb280a29957aa666b539231400d2495bfc6:        balance: 0 ether
```

TRAINING NOTES

---

92.   How to Mine a Pool for ETHs?

SSH into the AIHPC EC2 Server,

```
$ cd ~/eth/aipd
$ ./pool.sh
$ vi pool.sh
ethminer -F http://eth-eu.dwarfpool.com:80/0x502BeDb280a29957aa666B539231400d2495bfc6

{0x502BeDb280a29957aa666B539231400d2495bfc6 is MetaMask aipdcoin address}

{GPU Pool Mining}
#ethminer -G
-F http://eth-eu.dwarfpool.com:80/0x502BeDb280a29957aa666B539231400d2495bfc6

{ethminer options}
#ethminer –help
```

TRAINING NOTES

93.   How to Import the Main Account to MetaMask?

1. Get the main account: 0x1cd37d96b33f9ad2f232e9f280305295025ce46a

```
ubuntu@ip-172-31-52-220:~/eth/aipd$ geth attach
Welcome to the Geth JavaScript console!

instance: Geth/v1.7.3-stable-4bb3c89d/linux-amd64/go1.9
coinbase: 0x1cd37d96b33f9ad2f232e9f280305295025ce46a
at block: 0 (Thu, 01 Jan 1970 00:00:00 UTC)
 datadir: /home/ubuntu/.ethereum
 modules: admin:1.0 debug:1.0 eth:1.0 miner:1.0 net:1.0 personal:1.0 rpc:1.0
txpool:1.0 web3:1.0

> loadScript("check.js")
true
> checkAllBalances()
0x1cd37d96b33f9ad2f232e9f280305295025ce46a:     balance: 0 ether
0x652b81f15f3e133077e632b3853b7fffd3e10ae7:     balance: 0 ether
0x502bedb280a29957aa666b539231400d2495bfc6:     balance: 0 ether
```

2. Get keystore locations

```
ubuntu@ip-172-31-52-220:~/eth/aipd$ geth account list
Account #0: {1cd37d96b33f9ad2f232e9f280305295025ce46a}
keystore:///home/ubuntu/.ethereum/keystore/UTC--2018-01-06T23-15-40.714567810Z--
1cd37d96b33f9ad2f232e9f280305295025ce46a
Account #1: {652b81f15f3e133077e632b3853b7fffd3e10ae7}
keystore:///home/ubuntu/.ethereum/keystore/UTC--2018-01-06T23-54-32.347283608Z--
652b81f15f3e133077e632b3853b7fffd3e10ae7
Account #2: {502bedb280a29957aa666b539231400d2495bfc6}
keystore:///home/ubuntu/.ethereum/keystore/UTC--2018-01-07T17-40-52.704794745Z--
502bedb280a29957aa666b539231400d2495bfc6
```

3. Import the keystore to MetaMask

4. TRAINING NOTES

94.   MetaMask Accounts for Geth & Pool Miner

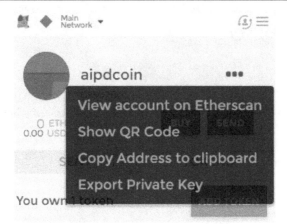

1. Get the MetaMask account address for **aipdcoin**

`0x502BeDb280a29957aa666B539231400d2495bfc6`

2. Export its private key as:
   `a8eb3e2c6404750d44565ec494f3d73a0c76902d1bb3067c82c6bb94ca6bfea6`

3. Creating a geth account by **importing** a private key

```
$ cd /home/ubuntu/eth/aipd
$ geth account import privkey1 {import to main network}
$ geth account import key3 --datadir /home/ubuntu/eth/aipd/ACPrivateChain
{import to aipd private network}
> checkAllBalances()
0x1cd37d96b33f9ad2f232e9f280305295025ce46a:    balance: 0 ether
0x652b81f15f3e133077e632b3853b7fffd3e10ae7:    balance: 0 ether
0x502bedb280a29957aa666b539231400d2495bfc6:    balance: 0 ether
```

4. Use `0x502bedb280a29957aa666b539231400d2495bfc6` to receive pool mining payment from the main network

   `~/eth/aipd$ vi pool.sh`

For geth account management, more at:

https://github.com/ethereum/go-ethereum/wiki/Managing-your-accounts

---

95. MetaMask to Use Private Network

---

1. MetaMask Custom RPC configuration

```
http://54.166.191.177:8545 for testrpc
http://54.166.191.177:9545 for truffle develop network
http://54.166.191.177:8555 for q2.sh
```

2. Get a new MetaMask account

```
acoin 1
address 0x833cb9657C32D580cABf2B3b76f6824cB8398EBd
private key=993f698ecf1a0783c0ebe0db97e0ed9e45dc49a97c0e66d2c182197e2b14bd6
pass=Oem123jcl$4
```

3. Import to private network

geth account import key3 --datadir /home/ubuntu/eth/aipd/ACPrivateChain

4. Transfer ETH to the new account

```
$ cd ~/eth/aipd
$ ./attach.sh
> checkAllBalances()
0x30bef62a6e9170f95b1dcb05659e133f85ce63a5:    balance: 78215 ether
0x833cb9657c32d580cabf2b3b76f6824cb8398ebd:    balance: 0 ether


>web3.eth.sendTransaction({from: '0x30bef62a6e9170f95b1dcb05659e133f85ce63a5', to:
'0x833cb9657c32d580cabf2b3b76f6824cb8398ebd', value: web3.toWei("2000",
"ether")});


> miner.start()
> checkAllBalances()
0x30bef62a6e9170f95b1dcb05659e133f85ce63a5:    balance: 28235 ether
0x833cb9657c32d580cabf2b3b76f6824cb8398ebd:    balance: 50000 ether
```

TRAINING NOTES

96.   Deploy ICO Contracts to Truffle Develop

Basic Truffle commands

```
$cd ~/eth/aipd/dapp/proj
$truffle migrate --network aipd
$truffle console
>networks
>migrate --reset
```

Truffle Develop to create accounts for MetaMask

```
$cd ~/eth/aipd/dapp/proj
$truffle develop {MetaMask can access accounts on http://54.166.191.177:9545}
Truffle Develop started at http://localhost:9545/

Accounts:
(0) 0x627306090abab3a6e1400e9345bc60c78a8bef57
(1) 0xf17f52151ebef6c7334fad080c5704d77216b732
(2) 0xc5fdf4076b8f3a5357c5e395ab970b5b54098fef
(3) 0x821aea9a577a9b44299b9c15c88cf3087f3b5544
(4) 0x0d1d4e623d10f9fba5db95830f7d3839406c6af2
(5) 0x2932b7a2355d6fecc4b5c0b6bd44cc31df247a2e
(6) 0x2191ef87e392377ec08e7c08eb105ef5448eced5
(7) 0x0f4f2ac550a1b4e2280d04c21cea7ebd822934b5
(8) 0x6330a553fc93768f612722bb8c2ec78ac90b3bbc
(9) 0x5aeda56215b167893e80b4fe645ba6d5bab767de

Private Keys: {Import these keys to MetaMask to create accounts with ETH balances}
(0) c87509a1c067bbde78beb793e6fa76530b6382a4c0241e5e4a9ec0a0f44dc0d3
(1) ae6ae8e5ccbfb04590405997ee2d52d2b330726137b875053c36d94e974d162f
(2) 0dbbe8e4ae425a6d2687f1a7e3ba17bc98c673636790f1b8ad91193c05875ef1
(3) c88b703fb08cbea894b6aeff5a544fb92e78a18e19814cd85da83b71f772aa6c
(4) 388c684f0ba1ef5017716adb5d21a053ea8e90277d0868337519f97bede61418
(5) 659cbb0e2411a44db63778987b1e22153c086a95eb6b18bdf89de078917abc63
(6) 82d052c865f5763aad42add438569276c00d3d88a2d062d36b2bae914d58b8c8
(7) aa3680d5d48a8283413f7a108367c7299ca73f553735860a87b08f39395618b7
(8) 0f62d96d6675f32685bbdb8ac13cda7c23436f63efbb9d07700d8669ff12b7c4
(9) 8d5366123cb560bb606379f90a0bfd4769eecc0557f1b362dcae9012b548b1e5

Mnemonic: candy maple cake sugar pudding cream honey rich smooth crumble sweet treat
```

Deploy AIPD contract to the develop network

```
>migrate -reset {deploy aipd contract to network 4447 and make available to 9545}
>networks
Network: develop (id: 4447)
  Migrations: 0x8cdaf0cd259887258bc13a92c0a6da92698644c0
  aipd: 0x345ca3e014aaf5dca488057592ee47305d9b3e10
```

97.   Private Blockchains for MetaMask Accounts

Create three private blockchains with accounts for MetaMask

```
Truffle develop {~/eth/aipd/dapp/proj}
    1)   start the private blockchain at http://localhost:9545/;
    2)   9545 is accessible to MetaMask accounts
    3)   Access through Truffle console

testrpc {~/eth/aipd/dapp/proj}
    1)   Start the private blockchain at http://localhost:8545/
    2)   8545 is accessible to MetaMask accounts
    3)   Access through: geth attach http://localhost:8545/

Networkid 20000616 {~/eth/aipd}

    1)   Run g1.sh, g2.sh {Terminal 1}
    2)   Access from: attach.sh {Terminal 2}
    3)   Accounts not yet accessible to MetaMask
```

4) TRAINING NOTES

98.   Truffle and Webpack

Webpack instructions

```
http://truffleframework.com/boxes/webpack

http://truffleframework.com/tutorials/building-testing-frontend-app-truffle-3
```

Install Webpack

```
$ cd ~/eth/aipd/dapp/proj1
$ truffle unbox webpack
$ truffle develop
>migrate -reset
>networks
Network: develop (id: 4447)
  ConvertLib: 0xfb88de099e13c3ed21f80a7a1e49f8caecf10df6
  MetaCoin: 0xaa588d3737b611bafd7bd713445b314bd453a5c8
  Migrations: 0x2c2b9c9a4a25e24b174f26114e8926a9f2128fe4
>test
```

Operate Webpack

```
Compile:             truffle compile
Migrate:             truffle migrate
Test contracts:      truffle test
Run linter:          npm run lint
Run dev server:      npm run dev
Build for production: npm run build
```

Web access

```
$ cd ~/eth/aipd/dapp/proj1
$ npm run dev
Project is running at http://localhost:8080/
```

```
Note:
    1)   Port 8080 must be open on EC2 security group dc2
    2)   replace localhost with the EC2 IP address
    3)   curl 8080 is good; Yet why node port 8080 not external?
```

TRAINING NOTES

99.   Externalize EC2 Webpack Node Server at 8080

1. Problem: EC2 port 8080 is open in Security Group dc2, the node web server cannot be accessible with EC2_IP:8080 externally; yet curl http://localhost:8080 is good.

2. Root case: webpack-dev-server just listens at "localhost" as opposed to "0.0.0.0"

3. Why?

```
ubuntu@ip-172-31-52-220:~/eth/aipd $ sudo netstat -pan | grep 80
tcp      0      0 127.0.0.1:8080        0.0.0.0:*      LISTEN    3350/node
tcp6     0      0 :::80                 :::*           LISTEN    1717/apache2

ubuntu@ip-172-31-52-220:~/eth/aipd/dapp/proj1$ nmap -p 8080 localhost
Host is up (0.000033s latency).
PORT      STATE SERVICE
8080/tcp open  http-proxy
```

Can't access node.js server from outside because it is listening on localhost IP i.e 127.0.0.1. So need to configure node.js to listen on 0.0.0.0 so it will be able to accept connections from all the IPs to the EC2 machine.

4. Solution for the truffle webpack dev server

```
$ cd ~/eth/aipd/dapp/proj1
$ vi package.json
dev is re-configured in package.json {adding --host 0.0.0.0} as
    "dev": "webpack-dev-server --host 0.0.0.0"
$ npm run dev
> truffle-init-webpack@0.0.2 dev /home/ubuntu/eth/aipd/dapp/proj1
> webpack-dev-server --host 0.0.0.0
```

5. Result: after restarting the dev server, the EC2 node server is accessible externally

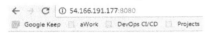

MetaCoin

Example Truffle Dapp

You have META

Send MetaCoin

Amount: e.g., 95
To Address: e.g., 0x93e66d9baea28c17d

[Send MetaCoin]

AIHPC® Cloud

100. Create and Get Account Balance in Truffle

1. Get Account Balance in Truffle

```
truffle(develop)> web3.eth.accounts
[ '0x627306090abab3a6e1400e9345bc60c78a8bef57',
  '0xf17f52151ebef6c7334fad080c5704d77216b732',
  '0xc5fdf4076b8f3a5357c5e395ab970b5b54098fef',
  '0x821aea9a577a9b44299b9c15c88cf3087f3b5544',
  '0x0d1d4e623d10f9fba5db95830f7d3839406c6af2',
  '0x2932b7a2355d6fecc4b5c0b6bd44cc31df247a2e',
  '0x2191ef87e392377ec08e7c08eb105ef5448eced5',
  '0x0f4f2ac550a1b4e2280d04c21cea7ebd822934b5',
  '0x6330a553fc93768f612722bb8c2ec78ac90b3bbc',
  '0x5aeda56215b167893e80b4fe645ba6d5bab767de' ]
truffle(develop)>  web3.eth.getBalance(web3.eth.accounts[0])
{ [String: '99917820100000000000'] s: 1, e: 19, c: [ 999178, 20100000000000 ] }
truffle(develop)>
```

2. Create new account and get balance in Truffle

```
truffle(develop)> web3.personal. web3.personal.newAccount
truffle(develop)> web3.eth.getBalance(web3.eth.accounts[0])
{ [String: '1000000000000000000000'] s: 1, e: 20, c: [ 1000000 ] }
```

3. Configure AIHPC EC2 server to hot and inline

```
$ cd ~/eth/aipd/dapp/proj1
$ vi package.json
"dev": "webpack-dev-server --hot --inline --host 0.0.0.0"
```

AIHPC® Cloud

101. Develop Dapp with Embark

https://github.com/iurimatias/embark-framework

Similar to Truffle, Embark is a framework that allows you to easily develop and deploy Decentralized Applications (DApps).

TRAINING NOTES

Copyright DeepCyber of Maryland, USA
Web: http://deepcybe.com | Email: demo@deepcybe.com

102.   Connect MetaMask to Private AIPD Blockchain

1. Start the AIPD private network in AIHPC EC2

```
$ cd ~/eth/aipd
$ ./g2.sh
```

2. Connect MetaMask to a private blockchain with 70,000+ ethers mined

```
      Critical! Added --rpcaddr="0.0.0.0" to ~/eth/aipd/g2.sh
$ cd ~/eth/aipd
$ cat g2.sh
geth --rpc --rpcport 8555 --rpcaddr="0.0.0.0" --datadir
/home/ubuntu/eth/aipd/ACPrivateChain --networkid 20000616 --rpccorsdomain="*"
--port "30303" --rpcapi "db,eth,net,web3" console
```

```
# https://github.com/ethereum/homestead-guide/blob/master/source/network/test-networks.rst
# --rpcaddr="0.0.0.0" allows the AIHPC EC2 private blockchain by geth to
listen to connection requests from all IPs as opposed to just connections
from the localhost
```

3. Add http://54.152.29.92:8555 to MetaMask for AIPD blockchain

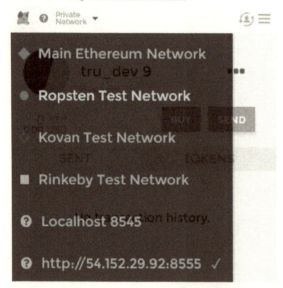

AIHPC® Cloud

103. Enable ETH Payment to Insurance Members

1. Check account balances with 70,000+ mined ethers at AIPD network

```
> loadScript("check.js")
true
> checkAllBalances()
0x30bef62a6e9170f95b1dcb05659e133f85ce63a5:    balance: 28235 ether
0x833cb9657c32d580cabf2b3b76f6824cb8398ebd:    balance: 50000 ether
```

2. Import base AIPD accounts as acoin 1 in MetaMask with 50,000 ethers to start

```
$ cd ~/eth/aipd/ACPrivateChain/keystore
$ vi UTC--2018-01-15T03-13-31.843425243Z--833cb9657c32d580cabf2b3b76f6824cb8398ebd
```

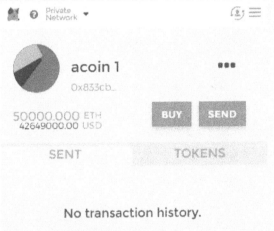

3. AIPD Payment happens in MetaMask Wallet: acoin 1 -> acoin 0 for 200 ETHs

Acion1 address = **0x833cb9657c32d580cabf2b3b76f6824cb8398ebd**

104. MetaMask ETH Transfer on Geth Console

```
> INFO [01-17|19:02:42] Submitted transaction
fullhash=0x48e13eb4f2e436a8514f875788d1ac6316e7d99535a0b1d6313744734a4e0a5c
recipient=0x833cb9657C32D580cABf2B3b76f6824cB8398EBd
INFO [01-17|19:07:19] Submitted transaction
fullhash=0xe47b05085c57cd5c49a07d8ab2a1c2bf82d14970ece87ef026e6f1857a2c56c0
recipient=0x833cb9657C32D580cABf2B3b76f6824cB8398EBd
INFO [01-17|19:08:49] Submitted transaction
fullhash=0x6345ed576341f68b06c8a8855ffc95cb1799b2856b4b8591e9a9d64413b257ef
recipient=0x833cb9657C32D580cABf2B3b76f6824cB8398EBd
INFO [01-17|19:08:52] Submitted transaction
fullhash=0xa9a727b57367c7cc0e977545b5bb83e7631652b3805f1616fdd7769315d64bab
recipient=0xc485677f00d13c8a6Ed424a4A5E137b87C812cbd
INFO [01-17|19:09:38] Submitted transaction
fullhash=0x9134faf5f9672d03b7261c263a575f213a5ce9210fff171c09b85d066021ebb7
recipient=0xc485677f00d13c8a6Ed424a4A5E137b87C812cbd

> miner.start()
INFO [01-17|19:16:43] Commit new mining work number=15673 txs=0 uncles=0
elapsed=113.622µs
> checkAllBalances()
0x30bef62a6e9170f95b1dcb05659e133f85ce63a5:     balance: 28360.0000903 ether
0x833cb9657c32d580cabf2b3b76f6824cb8398ebd:     balance: 49499.9999097 ether
```

TRAINING NOTES

105. Transfer with Account Created in MetaMask

Compared to transferring ETHs from acoin 1 -> acoin 0, we see faster transaction to transfer ETHs to a new account that is created in MetaMask, i.e., acoin 2.

Instant transaction: *acoin 1-> acoin2 for 300 ETHs*

Delayed transaction - needs `miner.start()`: *acoin 1-> acoin0 for 200 ETHs*

TRAINING NOTES

106. Pre-allocate ETHs in AIPD network

Pre-allocate ETHs for an address in CustomGenesis.json {work in p24}

1. Remove the old datadir; then use command line to create a new account

```
$ cd ~/eth/aipd
$ rm -r ACPrivateChain
$ geth --datadir=./ACPrivateChain account new
Passphrase:
Repeat passphrase:
Address: {f0bcc7eec2ccbe673ab39b790165b5aff854d7d0}
```

2. Edit CustomGenesis.json with the new address – ad **0x** before the new address

```
$ vi CustomGenesis.json
{
    "config": {
        "chainId": 20000617,
        "homesteadBlock": 0,
        "eip155Block": 0,
        "eip158Block": 0
    },
    "difficulty": "0x400",
    "gasLimit": "0x8000000",
    "alloc":{
        "0xf0bcc7eec2ccbe673ab39b790165b5aff854d7d0":
        {"balance": "2000000000000000000000000000"}
    }
}
```

3. Run g1.sh and g2.sh

```
$ ./g1.sh
$ ./g2.sh
```

4. Check the account balance pre-allocated in CustomeGenesis.json

```
> loadScript("check.js")
true
> checkAllBalances()
0xf0bcc7eec2ccbe673ab39b790165b5aff854d7d0:      balance: 2000000 ether
```

107. Deploy a Smart Contract in Geth Console

https://medium.com/@gus_tavo_quim/deploying-a-smart-contract-the-hard-way-8aae778d4f2a

```
$ cd ~/eth/aipd/dapp/hcoin/contracts
$ vi hcoin.sol
$ sudo apt-get install -y solc
$ ../../g2.sh {Terminal 1 geth console >}
$ {Terminal 2} echo "var hcoinOutput=`solc --optimize --combined-json
abi,bin,interface hcoin.sol`" > hcoin.js
> loadScript("contracts/hcoin.js") {Terminal 1}
> hcoinOutput
> var hcoinContractAbi = hcoinOutput.contracts['hcoin.sol:hcoin'].abi
"[{\"constant\":false,\"inputs\":[{\"name\":\"data\",\"type\":\"uint256\"}],\
"name\":\"set\",\"outputs\":[],\"payable\":false,\"type\":\"function\"},{\"co
nstant\":true,\"inputs\":[],\"name\":\"get\",\"outputs\":[{\"name\":\"\",\"ty
pe\":\"uint256\"}],\"payable\":false,\"type\":\"function\"}]"
> var hcoinContract = eth.contract(JSON.parse(hcoinContractAbi))
> var hcoinBinCode = "0x" + hcoinOutput.contracts['hcoin.sol:hcoin'].bin

> personal.unlockAccount(eth.accounts[0])
> miner.start()

> var deployTransationObject = { from: eth.accounts[0], data: hcoinBinCode,
gas: 1000000 };
> eth.accounts[0]
"0x30bef62a6e9170f95b1dcb05659e133f85ce63a5" {coinbase_aipd in MetaMask}
> var hcoinInstance = hcoinContract.new(deployTransationObject)
> hcoinInstance
> eth.getTransactionReceipt(hcoinInstance.transactionHash);
> var hcoinAddress =
eth.getTransactionReceipt(hcoinInstance.transactionHash).contractAddress
> hcoinAddress

> var hcoin = hcoinContract.at(hcoinAddress)
> checkAllBalances()
0x30bef62a6e9170f95b1dcb05659e133f85ce63a5:    balance: 41800.0001323 ether
0x833cb9657c32d580cabf2b3b76f6824cb8398ebd:    balance: 49487.9998677 ether
> hcoin.get.call()
> hcoin.set.sendTransaction(42, {from: eth.accounts[0], gas: 1000000})
> hcoin.get.call()
```

AIHPC® Cloud

108.   Create ICO Contract hcoin.sol

```
$ cd ~/eth/aipd/dapp/hcoin/contracts
$ vi hcoin.sol
$ truffle develop
>migrate
>test
>hcoin.deployed().then(function(instance) { app = instance; })




> checkAllBalances()
0x30bef62a6e9170f95b1dcb05659e133f85ce63a5:    balance: 43170.0001323 ether
0x833cb9657c32d580cabf2b3b76f6824cb8398ebd:    balance: 49487.9998677 ether
```

  Private Network ▾

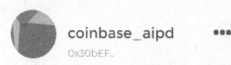

coinbase_aipd   •••
0x30bEF...

43075.000 ETH
41610450.13 USD

 BUY   SEND

 SENT   TOKENS

No transaction history.

109. Node and JavaScript Fixes

1. Fix async issues in solidity javascript test files (~/eth/aipd/dapp/aid/test) for lower node versions

```
sudo npm cache clean -f
sudo npm install -g n
sudo n stable
```

2. Fix import and export code

```
Import -> Require
//import ether from '../helpers/ether';
var ether = require('../helpers/ether');


Export -> module.exports.
//export default function latestTime () {
function latestTime () {
  return web3.eth.getBlock('latest').timestamp;
}
module.exports.latestTime = latestTime;
```

3. Cannot find module 'chai'

```
$ sudo npm install -g mocha
$ npm install -g chai {}
```

TRAINING NOTES

110. Deploy to Rinkeby Light

1. Sync up a light rinkeby network

```
$wget https://www.rinkeby.io/rinkeby.json
$cd ~/eth/aipd
$geth --networkid=4 --datadir=$HOME/.rinkeby --syncmode=light --
ethstats='aipd_rink:Respect my authoritah!@stats.rinkeby.io' --
bootnodes=enode://a24ac7c5484ef4ed0c5eb2d36620ba4e4aa13b8c84684e1b4aab0cebea2
ae45cb4d375b77eab56516d34bfbd3c1a833fc51296ff084b770b94fb9028c4d25ccf@52.169.
42.101:30303?discport=30304 -rpc
```

2. Import coinbase address

```
$ cd ~/eth/aipd
$ geth account import --datadir /home/ubuntu/.rinkeby/geth/lightchaindata
key4
```

3. Unlock account { ~/eth/aipd/unlock.sh } or

```
$ geth --rinkeby --rpc --rpcapi db,eth,net,web3,personal --unlock
0x30bEF62A6e9170F95B1Dcb05659e133F85cE63A5 --datadir
/home/ubuntu/.rinkeby/geth/lightchaindata
```

4. Deploy smart contract including ico.sol from proj

```
$ cd ~/eth/aipd/dapp/proj {Terminal 2}
$ truffle migrate --network rinkeby
$ geth console --rinkeby --datadir /home/ubuntu/.rinkeby/geth/lightchaindata
> loadScript("../../check.js")
true
> checkAllBalances()
0x30bef62a6e9170f95b1dcb05659e133f85ce63a5:      balance: 2.23436972 ether
$ truffle console --network rinkeby
>networks
Network: rinkeby (id: 4)
  ConvertLib: 0x241866e698121a8dd8223bcc993bf9411977f88b
  MetaCoin: 0x3a9d270e2331cc873c2297ed0057577e6a01f9d8
  Migrations: 0x2d9ad5f68a5937ee9e11432fdd6645b2f2008560
  aipd: 0x6f75925d1f5608a84cbe6d239a10d5a40c503b7b
  hcoin: 0x51bca2c9808ecb1db800b483d2ca5c5d6ea3e3c5
  hcoin1: 0xcd159f4eda5b0c44dc5fc1f27cb13dec630a9991
  ico: 0x7c2150dac6e69774a523420d1cd9405dc23c5b69
```

5. Sources

- Deploy Truffle Deploy to Rinkeby:
  https://blog.abuiles.com/blog/2017/07/09/deploying-truffle-contracts-to-rinkeby/
- Connect to Rinkeby Light: https://www.rinkeby.io/#geth
- Import account: https://github.com/ethereum/go-ethereum/wiki/Managing-your-accounts

AIHPC® Cloud

111.   How to Request AIPD Ethers?

1.   Use a PC to set up and log into MetaMask (AIPD Wallet) on Chrome
https://chrome.google.com/webstore/detail/metamask/nkbihfbeogaeaoehlefnkodbef
gpgknn?hl=en -> Watch the HowTo video

2.   Custom RPC -> http://107.23.133.133:8555 -> Connect to the AIPD network

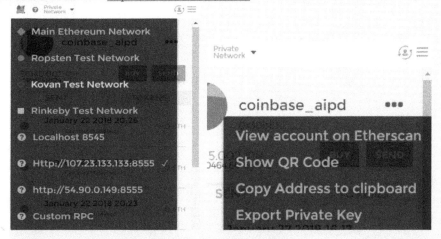

3.   Copy an account address from the private/AIPD network
4.   Send the account address to demo@deepcybe.com
5.   If approved by email, verify the account balance after the AIPD ethers are
transferred in a few minutes.

112.   Install Firefox AIPD Wallet on Android

1. Download **firefox** on Android devices (Huawei)
2. Install MetaMask add-on to Firefox browser
3. Set up MetaMask account
4. Add AIPD network to Custom RPC: `http://107.23.133.133:8555`
5. Transfer balances by the hash address of the account

TRAINING NOTES

113. Local: Build and Load AIPD Wallet to Chrome

1. Build the wallet in p24 ~/wallet

    1) `git clone https://github.com/yeswici/wallet`

    2) Install Node.js version 6.3.1 or later

    3) Install local dependencies with `cd ./wallet; npm install`

    4) Install gulp globally with `sudo npm install -g gulp-cli`

    5) Build the project to the ./dist/ folder with `gulp build`

    6) Optionally, to rebuild on file changes, run gulp dev.

    7) To package .zip files for distribution, run `gulp zip`, or run the full build & zip with gulp dist.

    8) Uncompressed builds can be found in /dist, compressed builds can be found in /builds once they're built.

    9) FTP from p24 to C:\Ethereum\MetaMaskExtension\zip\metamask-chrome-3.13.5

2. Load the wallet to Chrome

    10) Visit chrome://extensions (via omnibox or menu -> Tools -> Extensions).

    11) Enable Developer mode by ticking the checkbox in the upper-right corner.

    12) Click on the "Load **unpacked extension**..." button.

    13) Select the directory containing your unpacked extension:
    C:\Ethereum\MetaMaskExtension\zip\metamask-chrome-3.13.5

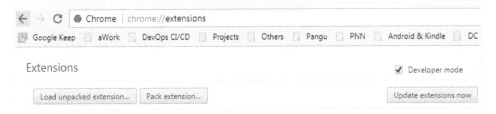

114. Test Crowdsale.sol/ico.sol with the Wallet

1. Introduction

Remix and Wallet: https://karl.tech/learning-solidity-part-1-deploy-a-contract/

https://github.com/ethereum/go-ethereum/wiki/Contract-Tutorial

2. Source code in /home/ubuntu/eth/aipd

```
Crowdsale.sol
ico.sol
```

3. Code deployed/ran in Remix:

https://ethereum.github.io/browser-solidity/#optimize=false&version=soljson-v0.4.19+commit.c4cbbb05.js

4. Deployed with Remix and Wallet

chrome-extension://nkbihfbeogaeaoehlefnkodbefgpgknn/popup.html

5. Testing in EC2

```
$ cd /home/ubuntu/eth/aipd
$ vi Crowdsale.sol
$ vi test.sh
$ echo "var crowdsaleCompiled =`solc --optimize --combined-json
abi,bin,interface Crowdsale.sol`" > Crowdsale.js
```

TRAINING NOTES

115.   Valuations for Qeth Network and Blockchain

Revenue models	Annual Sales	Total for 10 years
ETH on Qeth chain network	40,000/$34M	$340M (400,000 ETH)
High-speed miner cluster on AIHPC	$100M /sell 2 miner clusters per year	$1,000 M ($50M per cluster)
Global pay like Ripple for for-good businesses (smart contracts/ICO/coins)	Operating revenue expected $2 million per year	$20M
	$136 M	**$1,360,000 Million**

Notes:
1.   ETH: 400,000 X $857 (coinbase as of 2/12) = $342,800,000 ($340 M)
     Assume we sell 1/10 (40000 ETH) per year; annual revenue is $34 M
2.   High-speed miner cluster: requested by China's potential clients to
     price at $50M a cluster on location restrictions – assume we sell 2
     miner cluster per year so annual revenue is $100M
3.   Global pay like Ripple for for-good businesses -> operating revenue
     expected $2 million per year.

1. Invest like ETH; **400k QETH** mined by high-speed ETH miners; accessible by ETH wallet; technically ready for exchanges (Binewex.com, Gate) targeting QETH/ETH=1

2. **High-speed ETH miners** by AIHPC/Amazon platform, compared to regular GPU ETH miners

AIHPC® Cloud

3. QETH is **Safer** than common ETH; Quantum security built into the Qeth blockchain to secure QETH from quantum attacks by salting SHA-256 hashes with quantum keys

Security

Quantum computers could crack Bitcoin, but fixes are available now

Shor, we need a new sig scheme

By Richard Chirgwin 9 Nov 2017 at 03:45   10 💬   SHARE

An international group of quantum boffins reckons Bitcoin could be broken by the year 2027.

4. Global pay like **Ripple** for charity/for-good/SeniorCare project

5. **Mother network and ETH** for new smart contracts/coins/ICOs for charity/SeniorCare projects – mdaiac.com, fintech4good.co – see tokens in the wallet

116. TChain Hardware Wallet: Send Token Error

Problem: send LCAI token from Wallet A (tokenbase) -> Wallet B (Account 1) failed

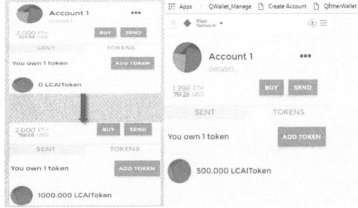

tokenbase holds 100,000,000 LCAIToken and all other new TCH tokens

Root cause: MyEtherWallet plugin of Wallet A was disabled

Fix: enable the plugin after clicking the icon

TRAINING NOTES

AIHPC® Cloud

117. What are the addresses for tokenbase wallet and new TCH tokens?

1. Tokenbase holds all TCH new tokens, wallet address is
   0xD35484b4f77695d7269B237C03cF598bd5474754

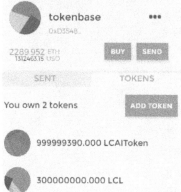

2. TCH Token addresses (see thetchain.com)
   LCL contract address: 0x60977e90803a0623ad1f9350db45c7ddf96e2dde
   TCHW (hardware wallet) contract address:
   0x1f400cc9a0f5307056568f38ad93d47992b143cf
   TCHE (EOS supernode HPC cloud cluster) contract address:
   0x037b036eea2ec0bf86b0e073433d630ad3d15447

Symbol	Size	Notes	Contract address
MAY	300m	Maytown retirement, $1B+ real estate investment	0xbaa00958e2ecedb535e6b07999132bb3fb2ebb38
TCH	300m	TChain, $150m valuation, FinTech	0xbe4c834c4d952bf7f34abf4080c92378fbc6088d
LCAI	1B	Lung Cancer AI Prevention, PI of Hopkins Med School	0x6e2ae49e3b1b737da433b191eece91c17fe4b624
DMA	100m	Digital Medical Asset, Hopkins PhD	0x06d10d1ee55158c4c500259f38f0e3de11551fe4
DBO	1B	Doctor Bot for Weight Loss, Artificial brain and Watson NLP	0xc2cdde46c95dee92e9b8aaeb09bf1cfebf1cf74a
MBC	1B	Mobile BlockChain, MBC chip, Princeton PhD	0x15d62356d2fa4adff89f4fcee554411f28c7ee0c

AIHPC® Cloud

118. EOS Docker Install

https://github.com/EOSIO/eos/wiki/Local-Environment#runanode

Docker
Simple and fast setup of EOSIO on Docker is also available. You can find up to date information about EOSIO Docker in the Docker Readme.

Install Dependencies

- Docker Docker 17.05 or higher is required

Build EOSIO image
```
$ git clone https://github.com/EOSIO/eos.git --recursive
$ cd eos/Docker
$ docker build . -t eosio/eos
```

Start nodeos docker container only
```
$ docker run --name nodeos -p 8888:8888 -p 9876:9876 -t eosio/eos start_nodeos.sh
arg1 arg2
```

By default, all data is persisted in a docker volume. It can be deleted if the data is outdated or corrupted:

```
$ docker inspect --format '{{ range .Mounts }}{{ .Name }} {{ end }}' nodeos
fdc265730a4f697346fa8b078c176e315b959e79365fc9cbd11f090ea0cb5cbc
$ docker volume rm fdc265730a4f697346fa8b078c176e315b959e79365fc9cbd11f090ea0cb5cbc
```
Alternately, you can directly mount host directory into the container

```
$ docker run --name nodeos -v /path-to-data-dir:/opt/eos/bin/data-dir -p 8888:8888 -p
9876:9876 -t eosio/eos start_nodeos.sh arg1 arg2
```

Get chain info
```
$ curl http://127.0.0.1:8888/v1/chain/get_info
```

Start both nodeos and keosd containers
```
$ docker-compose up
```
After `docker-compose up`, two services named nodeos and keosd will be started. nodeos service will expose ports 8888 and 9876 to the host. keosd service does not expose any port to the host, it is only accessible to cleos when runing cleos is running inside the keosd container as described in "Execute cleos commands" section.

Execute cleos commands
You can run the `cleos` commands via a bash alias.

AIHPC® Cloud

```
$ alias cleos='docker-compose exec keosd /opt/eos/bin/cleos -H nodeos'
$ cleos get info
$ cleos get account inita
```
Upload sample exchange contract

```
$ cleos set contract exchange contracts/exchange/exchange.wast
contracts/exchange/exchange.abi
```
If you don't need keosd afterwards, you can stop the keosd service using

```
$ docker-compose stop keosd
```

Change default configuration
You can use docker compose override file to change the default configurations. For example, create an alternate config file config2.ini and a docker-compose.override.yml with the following content.
```
version: "2"

services:
  nodeos:
    volumes:
      - nodeos-data-volume:/opt/eos/bin/data-dir
      - ./config2.ini:/opt/eos/bin/data-dir/config.ini
```
Then restart your docker containers as follows:

```
$ docker-compose down
$ docker-compose up
```

Clear data-dir
The data volume created by docker-compose can be deleted as follows:

```
$ docker volume rm docker_nodeos-data-volume
```

119. EOS Native and EOS Wallet – Dawn 3.0

Start EOS

```
~/eos/bin/starteos.sh
nodeos -e -p eosio --plugin eosio::wallet_api_plugin --plugin eosio::chain_api_plugin
--plugin eosio::account_history_api_plugin --http-server-address 0.0.0.0:8888
```

Create a wallet

```
cd ~/eos/build/programs/cleos/
./cleos wallet create  # Outputs a password that you need to save to be able to lock/unlock the wallet

PW5J4dbBMsTQhQw5DbBZYGHxTgFueNDTKxcyJ9BpVgnJ8XsLRSHSN

ubuntu@ip-172-31-48-114:~/eos/build/programs/cleos$ cleos create key
Private key: 5KjtF9b3EN7Mz72nDRL13qfR9FQty7mXiexr8Vh1uhyTsgKHFaC
Public key: EOS6bmMQj4C9dhZYysTmFSjzEKz7uRrK3FX7oG8pj7MipCDZNwRap

ubuntu@ip-172-31-48-114:~/eos/build/programs/cleos$ cleos create key
Private key: 5HqPLiuftihwRDxvTSvkZD6H2xMqRw3GWrWL7EHfAvHHJ9HXxvw
Public key: EOS8ABEqcx5WTjWkFzkhCRtrDKRRNRaCJerEQDFSVTf2ihUKcTzE2

cleos wallet create -n tchain
Creating wallet: tchain
Save password to use in the future to unlock this wallet.
Without password imported keys will not be retrievable.
" PW5KjPLG9TaEk5j8EG8xuxmisV33DCD7zvFAPfu7PQByTC5LRQVpu "

cleos wallet unlock -n tchain

cleos wallet list

cleos wallet keys

cleos wallet import 5KjtF9b3EN7Mz72nDRL13qfR9FQty7mXiexr8Vh1uhyTsgKHFaC
```

TRAINING NOTES

120.   EOS Smart Contract

Load the Bios Contract

```
~/eos/build/programs/cleos$ cleos set contract eosio ~/eos/build/contracts/eosio.bios
-p eosio
Reading WAST...
Assembling WASM...
Publishing contract...
executed transaction:
5b531e2b60e5f528cf5d0f94635341583b005b2066ab8d9a665965b6c5dfbf35  3288 bytes  2200576
cycles
#          eosio <= eosio::setcode
{"account":"eosio","vmtype":0,"vmversion":0,"code":"0061736d0100000001581060037f7e7f0
060057f7e7e7e7e...
#          eosio <= eosio::setabi
{"account":"eosio","abi":{"types":[],"structs":[{"name":"set_account_limits","base":"
","fields":[{"n...
```

Create two Accounts: user, tester

```
cleos wallet keys
[[
    "EOS6MRyAjQq8ud7hVNYcfnVPJqcVpscN5So8BhtHuGYqET5GDW5CV",
    "5KQwrPbwdL6PhXujxW37FSSQZ1JiwsST4cqQzDeyXtP79zkvFD3"
],[
    "EOS77hjQEdc8BxZZrGujGGKFNJvw7FFMj1GJHTKwBwCbMV56DM4CX",
    "5JJsJXVoV9PK8m4a7uCF6xWMQXeCvvG8rduibLhrabjwriaHKD1"
],[
    "EOS8ZPGmRqnXJx7Xc4Fhrb2CMeDz1evGjmSPgMvv6KifXUoXwp2bg",
    "5K8GkxV3yEmbKwWbdAz3Wo71QWyvnoge8M2GyKJ5yecCWZatT9S"
]
]
cleos create account eosio user EOS6MRyAjQq8ud7hVNYcfnVPJqcVpscN5So8BhtHuGYqET5GDW5CV
EOS6MRyAjQq8ud7hVNYcfnVPJqcVpscN5So8BhtHuGYqET5GDW5CV

~/eos/build/programs/cleos$ cleos create account eosio tester
EOS77hjQEdc8BxZZrGujGGKFNJvw7FFMj1GJHTKwBwCbMV56DM4CX
EOS77hjQEdc8BxZZrGujGGKFNJvw7FFMj1GJHTKwBwCbMV56DM4CX
executed transaction:
509b212ec79c1bce9d21d4cfe0a152d62dec91bba8e0aae3e01e3d5364f3b6d2  352 bytes  102400
cycles
#          eosio <= eosio::newaccount
{"creator":"eosio","name":"tester","owner":{"threshold":1,"keys":[{"key":"EOS77hjQEdc
8BxZZrGujGGKFNJ...
```

121.EOS create token

```
cleos create account eosio eosio.token
EOS6MRyAjQq8ud7hVNYcfnVPJqcVpscN5So8BhtHuGYqET5GDW5CV
EOS6MRyAjQq8ud7hVNYcfnVPJqcVpscN5So8BhtHuGYqET5GDW5CV
```

Create token contract
```
cleos set contract eosio.token ~/eos/build/contracts/eosio.token -p eosio.token
```

Create token
```
cleos push action eosio.token create '[ "eosio", "1000000000.0000 EOS", 0, 0, 0]' -p
eosio.token
```

issue token to user
```
cleos push action eosio.token issue '[ "user", "100.0000 EOS", "memo" ]' -p eosio
```

TRAINING NOTES

AIHPC® Cloud

122.EOS RPC API

https://eosio.github.io/eos/group__eosiorpc.html#v1chaingetcode

http://eos.thetchain.com = http:// 34.226.76.22:8888

```
curl http://127.0.0.1:8888/v1/chain/get_info
```
http://eos.thetchain.com/v1/chain/get_info

```
curl http://127.0.0.1:8888/v1/chain/get_table_rows -X POST -d
'{"scope":"inita", "code":"currency", "table":"account", "json": true}'
```

http://eos.thetchain.com/v1//chain/get_table_rows -X POST -d '{"scope":"eosio",
"table":"user", "json": true}'

TRAINING NOTES

123.EOS Crashed and Cannot Relaunch

Fix: relaunch with **--resync**

```
nodeos -e -p eosio --plugin eosio::wallet_api_plugin --plugin
eosio::chain_api_plugin --plugin eosio::account_history_api_plugin  --http-
server-address 0.0.0.0:8888 --resync
```

Code location: ubuntu@ip-172-31-48-114:~/eos/bin$ vi ./starteos.sh

TRAINING NOTES

124. Imtoken for TChain

1. Installable on Apple: profile -> settings -> Web3 Setting -> Wallet service URL
2. Takes TChain web3 address: http://107.23.133.133:8555
3. Takes imported wallet on TChain to display QETH amount
4. Submit token TCHE to token@consenlabs.com

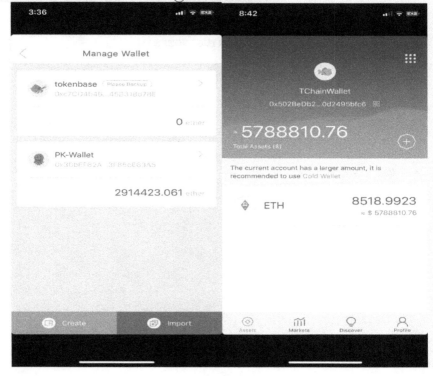

125. Why Security Analytics for Smart Contracts

Ethereum grant application:
https://docs.google.com/forms/d/1_Fi0UmsdYefkRmWZg12QJOQgQoEajAJPvJw1tRI9N0c/viewform?e
dit_requested=true&fbzx=-9115574763331629000

Concepts
1) Security analysis: analyze code for security risks and vulnerabilities
2) Security analytics: computer program and software to automate the analysis of code for security risks
3) Smart contracts: includes Ethereum and EOS code that may create new tokens as digital currencies
4) SOS - Secure Open Source: an AWS/DeepCyber cloud product on AWS marketplace for devops security
5) https://aws.amazon.com/marketplace/pp/B01N9MZQUM?qid=1526246513582&sr=0-1&ref_=srh_res_product_title

Problem:
Many Ethereum smart contracts are insecure, resulting in losses in millions of US dollars. For example, the hack to BEC (beauty chain) may have evaporated more than **two billion USD** worth of market value due to a bug in the smart contract written in Solidity. From its peak market cap of around 70 billion USD, BEC has gradually come down to around two billion USD as of April 22, when its trading value suddenly dropped to zero. It was discovered that hackers were able to exploit the BEC/SMT smart contracts and issue vigintillions (value with 63 zeros) of tokens to themselves.

How did BEC incident happen by the BatchOverflow Exploit?
Technically, there is a bug in the ERC 20 smart contract that issues and manages the crypto token. Let's use BEC as an example. (SMT is very similar.) The developer added a method called batchTransfer() to the contract. The method is intended to facilitate token transfer to multiple parties at once (i.e. a batch).

```
255    function batchTransfer(address[] _receivers, uint256 _value) public whenNotPaused returns (bool) {
256        uint cnt = _receivers.length;
257        uint256 amount = uint256(cnt) * _value;
258        require(cnt > 0 && cnt <= 20);
259        require(_value > 0 && balances[msg.sender] >= amount);
260
261        balances[msg.sender] = balances[msg.sender].sub(amount);
262        for (uint i = 0; i < cnt; i++) {
263            balances[_receivers[i]] = balances[_receivers[i]].add(_value);
264            Transfer(msg.sender, _receivers[i], _value);
265        }
266        return true;
267    }
268 }
```

Image credit from the CVE-2018–10299 security alert

However, the developer made a crucial mistake in the following line of code:
*uint256 amount = uint256(cnt) * _value*
The cnt here is the number of recipients to transfer the tokens to, the _value is the number of BECs each recipient should receive, and the amount is the computed amount the contract should withdraw from the sender's account for the transfer. Now, what if someone calls this batchTransfer function with a cnt * _value so large that the product exceeds the capability of the computer to keep track of 256 bit integer (uint256)? It will cause an infamous "buffer overflow," and cause the amount to compute to zero. Notice that both cnt and _value are legitimate unit256 numbers, but the amount is now zero. Hence you can

transfer _value number of BECs to anyone without withdrawing anything from the sender's account. So a sender with 1 BEC can now send trillions (in fact, vigintillions) of BECs to other recipients. More at https://cryptoslate.com/batchoverflow-exploit-creates-trillions-of-ethereum-tokens/

TSA (TChain Security Analytics)

- Is my token safe? BEC lost $2B due to the BatchOverflow attack to its smart contract code in April 2018.
- How to secure my token? 1) request TChain tokens 2) Run TSA on your smart contract - TSA analyzes ETH/EOS smart contracts for security vulnerabilities
- How is TSA built? See TSA design
- Email token@thetchain.com to request TChain tokens; more at thetchain.com

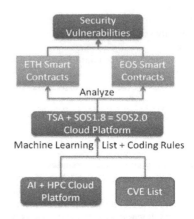

Symbol	Size	Notes	Contract address
MAY	300m	Maytown retirement, $1B+ real estate investment	0xbaa00958e2ecedb535e 6b07999132bb3fb2ebb38
TCH	300m	TChain, $150m valuation, FinTech	0xbe4c834c4d952bf7f34a bf4080c92378fbc6088d
LCAI	1B	Lung Cancer AI Prevention, PI of Hopkins Med School	0x6e2ae49e3b1b737da43 3b191eece91c17fe4b624
DMA	100m	Digital Medical Asset, Hopkins PhD	0x06d10d1ee55158c4c50 0259f38f0e3de11551fe4
DBO	1B	Doctor Bot for Weight Loss, Artificial brain and Watson NLP	0xc2cdde46c95dee92e9b8 aaeb09bf1cfebf1cf74a
MBC	1B	Mobile BlockChain, MBC chip, Princeton PhD	0x15d62356d2fa4adff89f4 fcee554411f28c7ee0c

126.   Solution – TChain Security Analytics

Solution to the cyber attacks to the Smart Contract

Security vulnerabilities of a token smart contract could be detrimental financially to token issuers and the reputation of Ethereum community. Millions of US dollars were stolen from investors and token owners by cyber attacks due to poorly coded smart contracts that lacked security analysis.

We are auditing TChain smart contracts with in-house TChain security analytics. Given the implication and magnitude of the security risks to Ethereum smart contracts, we are happy to share and build the in-house security analytics into the next release of AWS/DeepCyber SOS 2.0. The ethereum community shall be stronger in defending attacks to smart contracts by leveraging the smart-contract security analytics in SOS 2.0 that builds the security analytics into DevSecOps pipelines.

Install TSA on SOS 2.0 EC2 (on TChain EOS 34.226.76.22)
1. Build the docker image
   ```
   $ git clone https://github.com/ConsenSys/mythril/
   $ docker build mythril
   ```
2. Install from Pypi on Ubuntu
   ```
   $ sudo apt-get update
   $ sudo apt-get install -y software-properties-common
   $ sudo add-apt-repository -y ppa:ethereum/ethereum
   $ sudo apt-get update
   $ sudo apt-get install -y solc
   $ sudo apt-get install libssl-dev
   $ sudo apt-get install -y python3-pip=9.0.1-2 python3-dev
   $ sudo ln -s /usr/bin/python3 /usr/local/bin/python
   $ sudo apt-get install -y pandoc
   $ sudo apt-get install -y git
   $ sudo pip3 install mythril
   ```
   If you plan to analyze Solidity code you'll also need the native version of solc at http://solidity.readthedocs.io/en/v0.4.21/installing-solidity.html#binary-packages. Solcjs is not supported.

TSA 1) solves the pain points of mythril installation; 2) extends TSA/myth to DevOps pipeline
1. Environment setup for **pip3** python3 mythril libs
   ```
   python3.6 -m pip -V
   ```
2. Incompatible **conda** lib
   ```
   conda install -c anaconda cytoolz
   ```
3. **Cytoolz** version issue

127.   ETH TChain Security Analytics (TSA) in SOS2.0

TSA extends myth to SOS cloud to form SOS2.0. How to use TSA for Ethereum smart contracts?

1. **SSH into the SOS 2.0 EC2 (TChain EOS 34.226.76.22)**, then

```
cd ~/devsecops/tsa
ubuntu@ip-172-31-48-114:~/devsecops/tsa$ ./tsa
usage: tsa [-h] [-g GRAPH] [-x] [-t] [-d] [-j OUTPUT_FILE] [-c BYTECODE]
           [-a CONTRACT_ADDRESS] [-l] [-o <text/json>] [--verbose-report]
           [--init-db] [-s EXPRESSION] [--hash SIGNATURE]
           [--storage INDEX,NUM_SLOTS,[array] / mapping,INDEX,[KEY1, KEY2...]]
           [--solv SOLV] [-m MODULES] [--max-depth MAX_DEPTH]
           [--solc-args SOLC_ARGS] [--phrack] [--enable-physics]
           [-v LOG_LEVEL] [--leveldb LEVELDB_PATH] [-i]
           [--rpc HOST:PORT / ganache / infura-[network_name]]
           [--rpctls RPCTLS] [--ipc]
           [solidity_file [solidity_file ...]]

Security analysis of Ethereum smart contracts
```

2. **Verify good TChain smart contract code**

```
$ ./tsa -x solidity_examples/TCHE.sol
```

The analysis was completed successfully. **No issues were detected**.

3. **Detect bad smart contract with integer overflow**

```
$./tsa -x solidity_examples/ether_send.sol
```

==== Integer **Overflow** ====
Type: Warning
Contract: Crowdfunding
Function name: invest()
PC address: 501
A possible integer overflow exists in the function `invest()`.
The addition or multiplication may result in a value higher than the maximum representable integer.

      In file: solidity_examples/ether_send.sol:24
      balances[msg.sender] += msg.value

4. **Run TSA in DevSecOps CICD pipeline with SOS EC2 in a distributed architecture**
SOS Jenkins jobs remotely SSH into the EC2 to automate the security analytics on a regular basis

AIHPC® Cloud

128. Practicing TSA for EOS by SOS 2.0 Cloud

Concepts
1) TSA – TChain security analytics of SOS 2.0; Analyzes ETH and EOS smart contracts for security vulnerabilities
2) EOS code – includes the cpp code of the EOS base repo in the master branch and the specific cpp code for the EOS smart contracts
3) SOS 2.0 cloud – SOS v1.8 (DevOps security workflow) + TSA of the AWS EC2 instance
4) Goal: use SOS 2.0 cloud to analyze EOS code for security vulnerabilities

TRAINING NOTES

129. TChain Stick Wallet (TSW) 1.5 – Bootable Ubuntu Stick Wallet for Bitcoin Wallet

1. Install Bootable Ubuntu

https://tutorials.ubuntu.com/tutorial/tutorial-create-a-usb-stick-on-windows#1

HP-laptop c:\tchain – Ubuntu … iso, rufus

- A 2GB or larger USB stick/flash drive
- Microsoft Windows XP or later
- Rufus, a free and open source USB stick writing tool
- An Ubuntu ISO file. See Get Ubuntu for download links
- Launch Rufus
- Insert your USB stick
- Rufus will update to set the device within the **Device** field
- If the **Device** is incorrect, select the correct one from the device field's drop-down menu

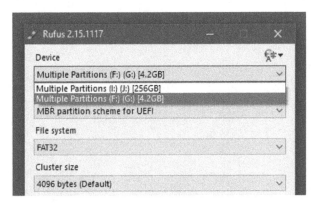

2. Install Bitcoin electrum

https://news.bitcoin.com/bitcoin-bank-less-thirty-minutes-usb-drive/

https://electrum.org/#download

Section 5: AI Cyber SaaS

130. AI Cyber Capabilities

Advanced AI cybersecurity containers (AISC) are developed and can be deployed on the AIHPC platform. After completing the AIHPC labs, email demo@deepcybe.com to request the AI Cyber capability summary and pricing data.

AISC ecosystem provides defensive and offensive AI Cyber capabilities to protect high value assets (HVA) for Cloud, enterprise, and IoT security.

Market Position

AISC_ML for ZTS

Use AI as machine learning algorithms to discover and deflect deep hidden vulnerabilities previously undefendable by traditional cybersecurity methodologies.

AISC AI GPU Chip

AISC™ Capabilities

AISC offers offensive and defensive AI cybersecurity capabilities by AI security containers and AI chips to protect high-value assets (HVA) in cloud, on premise, or IoT chips

AISC™ Ecosystem for AI Cyber

Sold By OCG (jmiller@ocg-inc.com | 646 326 7809)

AISC™ Overview

AI Security Containers (AISC™) Ecosystem for Defensive and Offensive AI Cyber capabilities for Cloud, Enterprise and IoT Security

Components of AISC™ Ecosystem

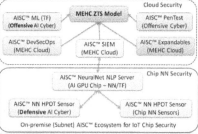

AISC DAC by NN/NLP for HVA Security

USPTO pending patent number 62843601

.·.·.AISC

Relevance

U.S. Executive Orders and Acts:
1) EO Cyber
2) EO AI (R&D priority)
3) IoT Cybersecurity Act
4) WH "Cloud First" Strategy

IoT Use Cases

AISC Components

TRAINING NOTES

---

131. How to Install AISC on AIHPC

For the cloud security edition of AISC,

1. Provision AIHPC instances from AWS Marketplace by following Topic 4: AIHPC is available in AWS GovCloud region for government users.

2. License AISC by contacting demo@deepcybe.com

3. Install AISC on AIHPC by AISC Get Started guide.

TRAINING NOTES

132. Summary

AIHPC book 350 extends AIHPC book 303 as follows:

1. Organizes the topics in five sections:

    1) AIHPC PaaS platform;

    2) AIHPC SaaS;

    3) blockchain security on AIHPC;

    4) blockchain labs on AIHPC;

    5) AI cyber SaaS on AIHPC.

2. Introduces the AI Cyber (AISC) SaaS capabilities on the AIHPC PaaS.

TRAINING NOTES

www.ingramcontent.com/pod-product-compliance
Lightning Source LLC
Chambersburg PA
CBHW031223050326
40689CB00009B/1449